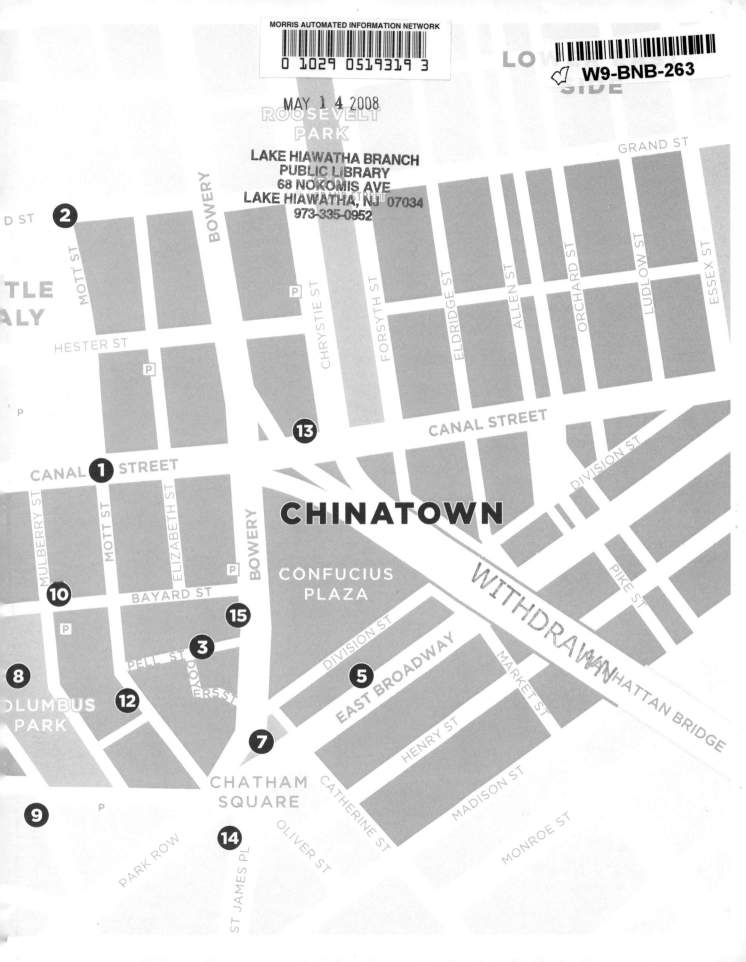

CHINA TOWN

NEW YORK

紐約國城

CHINA TOWN

NEW YORK

紐約中國城

PORTRAITS, RECIPES, AND MEMORIES

ANN VOLKWEIN

PHOTOGRAPHY BY VEGAR ABELSNES

COLLINS | DESIGN

An Imprint of HarperCollinsPublishers

Photography Credits

Courtesy of the Chinese Consolidated Benevolent Association: pages 8-9 (images 4, 10, 11, 16), 17, 64-65 (images 1, 4, 6, 8, 11, 12), 68.

Courtesy of Jan Lee: pages 8-9 (image 5, 12), 13, 43, 44, 45, 46 (bottom four images).

Courtesy of the Library of Congress, Prints and Photographs Division, reproduction numbers as follows: pages 8-9 (LC-USZ62-110967), 10-11 (image 2: LC-USZ62-41992, image 6: LC-DIG-ggbain-18320), 12 (LC-USZ62-120168), 14 (Detroit Publishing Company Collection, LC-D401-13646 and LC-USZ62-69696), 15 (LC-USZ62-69697), 16 (LC-DIG-ggbain-01554), 32 (LC-USZ62-72478), 70-71 (LC-DIG-ggbain-00025), 124-125 (LC-USZ62-62611), 134 (LC-DIG-ggbain-10143), 135 (LC-DIG-ggbain-10144).

All other photographs by Vegar Abelsnes.

CHINATOWN NEW YORK

For information, address HarperCollins Publishers, 10 East 53rd Street, New York, NY 10022.

HarperCollins books may be purchased for educational, business, or sales promotional use.
For information, please write:
Special Markets Department, HarperCollins Publishers, 10 East 53rd Street, New York, NY 10022.

FIRST EDITION

Designed by HSU + ASSOCIATES

Library of Congress Cataloging-in-Publication Data

Volkwein, Ann.
Chinatown, New York : portraits, recipes, and memories / by Ann Volkwein. — 1st ed.
p. cm.
Includes bibliographical references and index.
ISBN 978-0-06-118859-6
1. Chinatown (New York, N.Y.)—Description and travel. 2. Chinatown (New York, N.Y.)—Social life and customs. 3. Chinese Americans—New York (State)—New York—Social life and customs. 4. Community life—New York (State)—New York. 5. Chinese Americans—Food—New York (State)—New York. 6. Food habits—New York (State)—New York. 7. Cookery, Chinese. 8. New York (N.Y.)—Description and travel. 9. New York (N.Y.)—Social life and customs. I. Title.

F128.68.C47V65 2007
974.7'10444089951—dc22

2007027803

07 08 09 10 11 ◆/RRD 10 9 8 7 6 5 4 3 2 1

TO THE BRAVE AND INDUSTRIOUS IMMIGRANTS

WHO MAKE CHINATOWN GREAT.

CONTENTS

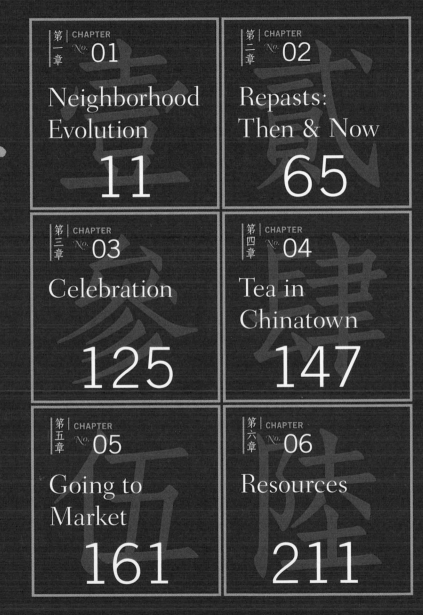

FOREWORD

中國城已成為娛樂地標

CHINATOWN HAS BEEN AN ENTERTAINMENT DESTINATION for New Yorkers in their own city as well as tourists for over 100 years, but the average New Yorker's knowledge of this busy, dense community is limited at best, often not going beyond the address of a favorite dim sum restaurant. The growing boundaries of the neighborhood are clear, but even though Chinese immigrants have been entering the United States in sporadic waves for 150 years, both the history and its current residents can seem obscure. This is not surprising, as Manhattan's Chinatown has a tradition of being a city unto itself, complete with governing bodies, unique marketplaces, and territorial boundaries.

But what is Chinatown today? Dr. Joseph Lee, associate professor of history at nearby Pace University, suggests, "Chinatown is a very flexible idea, rather than a territory or space. New Chinese immigrants go there when they need to do business, as a business outpost." The work of Hunter College professor Peter Kwong reveals the overall trend toward the suburbanization of Chinatowns, from New Jersey to San Gabriel, California. In fact, "ethnoburbs" may be where Chinese Americans are heading in general in the United States. Having seen these new areas develop across the country, one gets the impression that Chinatowns in America are becoming moveable feasts of culture, for while they may not have pagoda roofs and chinoiserie to announce their presence, they can still be recognizable—and sometimes as small as a strip mall with a collection of restaurants, an herbal shop, and a market selling lotus root.

This book is an introduction and a guide to Manhattan's Chinatown, to its historical and current cultural pathways and traditions, as well as a cultural snapshot, a window into the people who continue to give life to the streets and shops and restaurants of the neighborhood. Food is a major, integral part of life in Chinatown, and thus plays a large role in these pages. At every turn, fruits burst from street carts, vegetables and seafood seem to tumble out from even the shallowest storefront—not to mention the more than 500 restaurants in the neighborhood. And while Asian ingredients, products, and vegetables are more and more widely available, nowhere

前言

are they as reasonably priced or as abundant as they are in Chinatown. The Repasts and Going to Market sections are meant to demystify some of the more unusual finds in the neighborhood for cooks and visitors alike.

Despite the trends toward suburbanization and the growing popularity of Chinatowns in the outer boroughs of New York itself, with the efforts of the people profiled here, among many others, Manhattan's Chinatown continues to evolve as a home for first-time immigrants and as a center and a symbol of Chinese cultural life and history in the United States. As Dr. Lee eloquently expresses, "Chinatown can be anywhere in the U.S. or outside the U.S. But for the Chinese community, in order for them to understand what Chinese culture means, I think they need to have a sense of a geographical space that they can walk, that they can feel, that they can touch. New York's Chinatown as an idea as well as a community is continuing to develop, so this book captures a particular moment in Chinatown history, at the beginning of the twenty-first century." ○

1
2

CHAPTER

第一章 *No.* 01

壹

PRINTING

146 · A.M. PORTER · 146

148 A.M. PORTER
POWER
PRINTING
STORE

5
6
9 10

SOY KEE CO., 7-9 Mott Street, New York.

tonight and su
now expected to
chose to tell you
when I return

DEDICATED TO THE
RESTORATION OF THE
TRANSFIGURATION CHURCH
1997
NO FOOD FUNERAL SERVICES
25 MULBERRY STREET
NEW YORK, N.Y. 10013
真福聖殿

16 17

Neighborhood Evolution

FROM TOP LEFT: 1. On the left is Edward Mooney House, at the corner of Pell and Bowery, named after the butcher who built it in 1785. It is the oldest townhouse in New York City. 2. A view looking south on Mott. Port Arthur Restaurant was one of the most popular restaurants in Chinatown in the early twentieth century. 3. Layered signs reveal vestiges of the neighborhood's past. 4. Note the subway and elevated instructions on the cover of this Port Arthur Restaurant menu. 5. Jan Lee's mother in a classic 1950s pose with an appliance. 6. A printing company façade in the early 1900s. 7. Items on display at the Museum of Chinese in the Americas (MoCa). 8. The Chinese Consolidated Benevolent Association façade flying the Republic of China flag. 9. A sewing machine on display at the MoCa. 10. Soy Kee, located below the Port Arthur Restaurant, sold porcelain, housewares, gifts, and supplies. 11. "Such sights I never expected to see," writes an impressed tourist on a postcard in 1910. 12. Jan Lee's father playing stickball in 1936. 13. Rev. Raymond Nobiletti outside the Church of the Transfiguration. 14. A view of Chinatown looking west, north, and east from the roof of 11 East Broadway. 15. The doorway to the Fukien American Association. There are more than 150 Fujian associations alone. 16. One of the Port Arthur dining rooms. 17. In this photo on display at MoCa, families lay incense, flowers, and food offerings on their family members' graves during Qing Ming, or "tomb sweeping" day. This holiday celebrates spring and honors ancestors. 18. The main staircase at the Chinese Consolidated Benevolent Association, 62-64 Mott Street. 19. The interior of Eastern States Buddhist Temple, 64 Mott Street. 20. This is Wah Wing Sang funeral home at 26 Mulberry. The names posted on the door indicate the current list of the deceased to whom you can pay your respects. The funeral homes along Mulberry are a vestige of the Lower East Side. They started out as Italian, but funeral home licenses are difficult to obtain, and as the neighborhood changed they were simply sold to the Chinese. To this day, an Italian funeral band is often used during Chinatown funerals. Perhaps a strange sight and sound in context, but it was traditional to have music at funerals in China—and the community adapted.

Children and families were a rare sight in Chinatown until the mid-twentieth century due to strict immigration quotas and work visas. Even prior to the 1882 Exclusion Act, women and children rarely emigrated. The majority of male immigrants came from poverty-stricken areas of southern China to the West Coast, seeking fortunes to bring back to China.

THE NEIGHBORHOOD

鄰里

Becoming Chinatown

中國城的演變

THE SECTION OF MANHATTAN'S LOWER EAST SIDE that is now called Chinatown has gone through transitions that reflect major immigration waves in the city. First came the Dutch settlers, laying claim to what was known to the Canarsie Indians as Werpoes Hill; then there were the Irish in the gang-infested Five Points era, followed by the Italian and the Jewish communities.

The Collect Pond was located where Columbus Park is today. Tanneries and butchers on Mott and Bayard Streets would dump carcasses into the waters, creating a haven for disease. The city drained it in 1810, digging a canal which was later covered over and named Canal Street. Having been brought to the attention of the city by social reformers, the unhealthy living conditions of the tenements were so severe that they were torn down, and the park was created in 1890. Originally Mulberry Bend Park, it was later renamed Columbus Park, in honor of the neighborhood's Italian residents.

In the late nineteenth and early twentieth centuries, as the Chinese population grew, tongs, or merchant and trade organizations were set up as general arbiters for disputes. Protection from a tong was often key to survival for merchants, who couldn't rely on the police, and tongs played an enforcement role in the community from a business and personal perspective. "Most complaints were commercial," explains one longtime resident. "Commercial renters registered with a tong, paying 'key money,'

RIGHT: A view down Doyers Street from Pell. The billboard on the wall on the right was a focal point for the neighborhood, news from China, the war, community announcements—everything was posted here, as an erstwhile community newspaper. BELOW: Doyers Street looking from the Bowery, early twentieth century.

Police detectives surveying China-town during early tong wars.

COMING TO THE MOUNTAIN OF GOLD

Escaping extreme poverty in southern China during and after the bloody Taiping Rebellion (1850 to 1865), Chinese men were drawn to the United States, or the "Mountain of Gold," to seek fortunes for their families. The first wave was attracted by the California gold rush of the 1850s, and the second wave, some forcibly recruited as laborers, came to build the Transcontinental Railroad. The railroad was completed in 1869, at which time thousands of male Chinese laborers were suddenly out of work. Anti-Chinese sentiment had grown, particularly on the West Coast, during the 1870s when the country experienced a post–Civil War depression. Competition for jobs was fierce, and Americans began to desire work that earlier only the Chinese had wanted, such as running laundries. In this climate of persecution, the 1882 Exclusion Act was passed, strictly prohibiting Chinese immigration. It was in this period that the Chinese began to move east, seeking refuge and work. This movement eventually formed the early "bachelor societies" of Chinese men in what became New York's Chinatown, as women were rarely found among the immigrant laborers. Due to China's allied status in World War II, the Chinese Exclusion Act was repealed by President Roosevelt in 1943—but the yearly immigration quota was set at only 105. Large numbers of Chinese Americans actively enlisted during World War II, and in 1946 the War Brides Act finally permitted 6,000 wives of Chinese servicemen to enter the United States. The boost in the population of the neighborhood, and the presence of more families and children, would not be significant until after 1965 when racial quotas for immigrants were finally abolished. The 1882 Exclusion Act is the only chapter in Title 8 of the U.S. Code that has ever been specific to a nationality or ethnic group.

which was the only way to guarantee a lease. Soon apartm done the same way. Each tong had their own territory." The survived by running lotteries and gambling houses. On L located on Mott Street, was the first, representing or protecti followed by Hip Sing on Pell Street, representing the merc community suffered from a spate of tong wars that starte and lasted, in waves through the early thirties. Both organi started in other cities, so when the tongs were at war, the repercussions across the country. Youth gangs began in the and eventually became more associated with tongs, bec violent in the seventies and into the eighties. According t whose cousin was the head of a gang, there was a code until the mid-eighties, when informants began speaking o no longer safe to be associated with a gang. The On Leo and Tong On leaders, groups controlled gangs up until the when the federal government finally cracked down under Influenced and Corrupt Organizations Act (RICO).

Doyers Street runs from Pell to the Bowery, with a the middle. While some say it was designed that way b community, who believed it was auspicious as ghosts can straight line, the street was originally the driveway to a h by a Mr. Heinrich Doyer. Today, the site of Coco Fashion Chinese opera theater, where men of the "bachelor soci of the twentieth century would spend their leisure tin

would visit. Another piece of Chinatown lore is that there was a secret escape route used by gang members through the door to the right of the theater.

If you take the "secret" passageway today, you're taken down steps and through the building, passing by employment agencies, herbalists, and empty shops, until you end up on the Bowery in the lobby of the Wing Fat Mansion building.

ASSOCIATIONS

工會聯盟 **CHINESE ASSOCIATIONS HAVE BEEN A PART OF LIFE** in the Chinese American community from the very beginning in the mid-nineteenth century, when the first major influx of immigrants from China came to San Francisco. In San Francisco, associations, which were formed based on family names and provinces, would call out to the arriving passengers in their dialect, then shuttle them back to the association to help them assimilate and survive.

Of the more than 1,000 associations in New York's Chinatown, the largest is the Chinese Consolidated Benevolent Association (CCBA). Founded in 1883, it has served as an umbrella organization for smaller associations. Some are clan-based, such as the Lee, Eng or Chan family

associations, or provincial, such as the Hoy Sun Yeung (where most early immigrants came from) and Lin Sing (representing those from outside Hoy Sun) associations. They also include political organizations such as the Kuo Min Tang (Nationalist Party) Eastern Regional Office, and professional and trade organizations such as the Chinese Chamber of Commerce and the Chinese American Restaurant Association, as well as religious and cultural organizations. There are sixty member associations today.

From the beginning, the role of the organization was quasi-governmental, both within the community and eventually as a voice for the community in New York City politics. The CCBA was where people went to settle disputes within the community, and the president of the CCBA was historically referred to as "the mayor of Chinatown." Despite its long history and influence in the community, in 1954 Robert F. Wagner was the first mayor of New York to visit the CCBA.

The organization grew to include schools after 1945. Today they run the largest Chinese school in the eastern United States, as well as a daycare center on Division Street. The Association supports its members in efforts to integrate into American society, provides social services such as voter registration, leads charitable and recreational endeavors, and maintains ties to other Chinese groups.

Over the years, CCBA has taken action on behalf of the community. For example, they led a 10,000-strong silent protest in front of City Hall in 1982 when the city wanted to build a new prison in Chinatown. In the end, a compromise was reached wherein the city also built a senior citizens' center and shopping mall at the edge of the building site. To this day they hold a monthly meeting on the status of the community, attended by a representative of the Chinatown police precinct.

The CCBA supported Sun Yat-Sen from the beginning of his democratic movement in China, when China was under the Manchu rule. Meeting minutes recently uncovered reveal that he wrote the organization in 1911 asking for financial support. The CCBA rallied the community and wired him a $50,000 donation within a month. They continued to support the Republic of China after 1949, when Mao Tse-tung's Communist regime took over the country, and thus fly the Republic of China (Taiwan) flag over the roof of the building. In general, Chinatown is divided along the Bowery between "new" and "old" Chinatown. Old Chinatown, to the west, tends to be loyal to Taiwan, and flies that flag. New Chinatown consists of newer immigrants from mainland China, mainly Fujianese who live east of the Bowery, with

BELOW: A portrait of Dr. Sun Yat-Sen hangs in the CCBA. OPPOSITE: A gathering of the Chinese Reform Association, early twentieth century.

This statue of Lin Ze Xu, a nineteenth-century Fujianese hero who stood up against the British and was integral in starting the Opium Wars, faces up East Broadway toward "Little Fujian." To some not only is this appropriate, as it faces the most concentrated area of his fellow Fujianese, but its placement is also correct Feng Shui, facing the rising sun. To others it makes a political statement, as his back is toward Old Chinatown.

世界禁毒先驱林则徐
LIN ZE XU
1785-1850

PIONEER IN THE WAR
AGAINST DRUGS

East Broadway as their main thoroughfare instead of Mott. Associations that constitute this newer group fly the flag of the People's Republic of China. These two communities even run separate economies, side by side, with prices 10 to 25 percent less on the Fujianese side.

Associations are integral in the community for employers and job-seekers alike. If work or workers are needed, the network springs into action. Most associations also play a role in the community that is akin to a senior citizens' center. It's where they come to see friends, a home-away-from-home in Chinatown. At Tung On, members of the association play a form of Chinese dominos with the mah-jongg pieces, called *pai gao*, and 13-card poker for which you pay a nominal fee, per person, for each round.

Inside the Tung On Association, located at 17-19 Division Street, George Washington is hung on one side, Sun Yat-Sen on the other, with both the American flag and People's Republic of China flag represented.

Associations can get extremely specific—among the 1,000 that exist, there's an association for everyone. For example, the Cuban Chinese Benevolent Association resides on the third floor of 9 East Broadway. ○

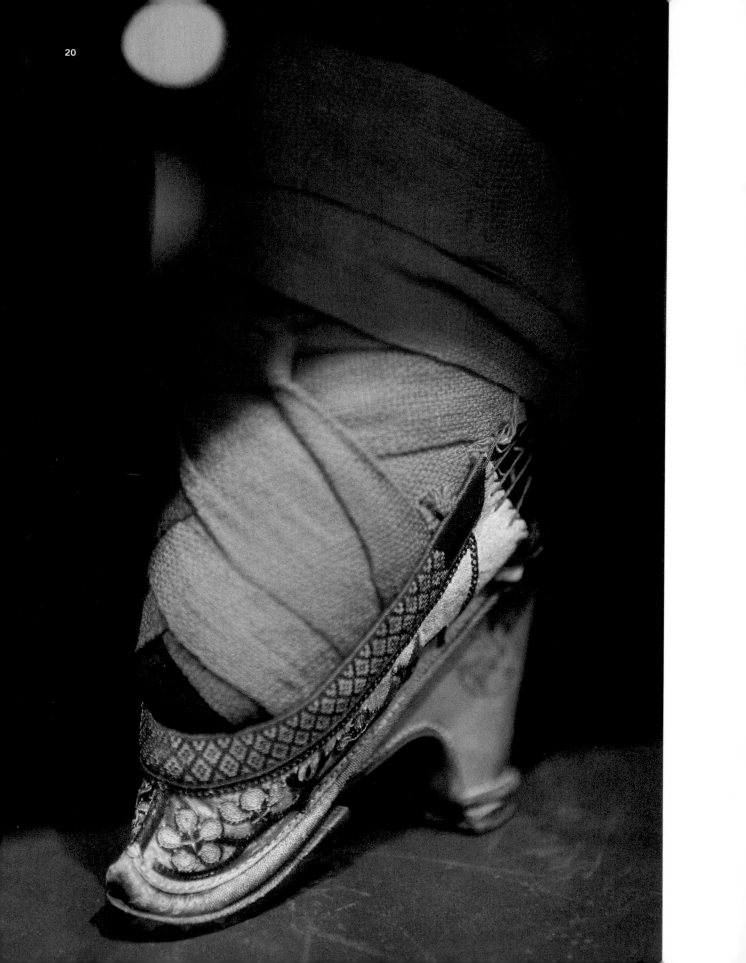

CAPTURING HISTORY

MUSEUM OF CHINESE IN THE AMERICAS, *211-215 Centre Street*

創建於一九八〇年

FOUNDED IN 1980 by John Kuo Wei Tchen and Charles Lai, the Museum of Chinese in the Americas (MoCA) strives to reclaim, preserve, and interact with the history of Chinatown in a manner that goes far beyond the static recitation of events or statistics, or even the collection of objects. Instead, its mission is to create a space in which a dialogue with history can occur. To this end it hosts programs including tours and lectures, captures oral histories of residents, former residents, and descendants of residents of Chinatown—and beyond, as it has expanded its reach to Chinese in the western diaspora. The Mapping Our Heritage Project exhibit encapsulates this approach, using an interactive virtual kiosk designed to capture statistical data, photos, oral histories, and artifacts about places within New York's historic Chinatown area. Visitors click on an address to see and hear information, and can also add their own thoughts or memories about Chinatown.

Architect Maya Lin has designed the new space on Centre Street, giving the museum the ability to work with a wider audience, as well as broadly rotate its collections. At 70 Mulberry, which had been its first home, they are planning to create a library and archive that will be an open research facility in the future.

The museum's collections reveal milestones in Chinese American history and preserve personal connections to the events. For example, a sewing machine on exhibit represents the scores of garment factory workers who came out of the Chinese community. The influx of immigrants from Hong Kong and Taiwan in the seventies and eighties provided a steady stream of workers, particularly women, into New York sweatshops. As overseas factories took over garment manufacturing in the eighties, Chinatown entrepreneurs were credited with saving New York's garment industry. To this day, 70 percent of all clothing manufactured in New York is produced by Chinese- and Korean-owned factories. ○

TOP: This collection of letters and war memorabilia tells a tale of longing for home, East and West. OPPOSITE: A child-size shoe meant to have been worn by a woman who had her feet bound most of her life, so as to remain tiny. This debilitating practice was followed as small feet were considered attractive in Imperial China. P. T. Barnum was among the first to bring this practice to New Yorkers' attention, displaying a Chinese woman, Miss Pwan-Ye-Koo, with bound feet less than three inches long, as a "curiosity" at his museum in the mid-nineteenth century.

紐約中國城 | **CHINATOWN NEW YORK**

23 二十三

哥倫比亞公園

晨曦時刻

COLUMBUS PARK

IN THE EARLY MORNING HOURS, almost every corner of the park is dotted with gracefully moving tai chi practitioners. They follow in unison the same set of movements, usually with one person leading. Young and old arrive for this ritual, but as the exercise is gentle on joints, the practice of tai chi is particularly popular with the elderly. Tai chi has different families and forms of practice. One is the sword dance. Yet another recreation and discipline incorporates a fan. The fan is associated with *yuen ji*, a dance form of martial art meant for health and exercise, utilizing smooth, graceful movements.

Sometimes you can catch a group of Cantonese men at one bend in the park, sitting by their bird cages, hung on tree branches around them. They value the birds as much as they do their children, says one Chinatown native; it's considered a vice—but a good vice because it's not gambling. These rare, valuable birds are hand fed, and music is played to them in the wintertime so they don't forget how to sing. ○

LEFT: Chinese chess played out under the trees. Intense competition and concentration typify these matches on a daily basis. **RIGHT:** Musicians play traditional instruments, and passersby come to sing along with them.

信仰 FAITH

追溯巷弄間

TRACING CHINATOWN'S STREETS through Jewish, Irish, Italian, and Chinese roots are landmarks to faith, found sprinkled throughout the neighborhood.

THE CHURCH OF THE TRANSFIGURATION, 29 *Mott Street*

OPPOSITE LEFT: Interior of the Church of the Transfiguration. ABOVE LEFT: The Shearith Israel Cemetery on St. James Place. Just off Chatham Square on an elevated piece of land, this is the oldest Jewish cemetery in New York. It is also the oldest standing artifact to be found in the city. The first American-born rabbi is buried there, as well as eighteen Jewish soldiers of the Revolutionary War. ABOVE RIGHT: Located next to the Fujian community's Puchao Buddhist temple, the Eldridge Street Synagogue is a registered national landmark.

FATHER NOBILETTI, OR "FATHER RAY" AS HE IS KNOWN, has been at the Church of the Transfiguration since 1991. Full of life and passionate about his calling, he muses on history, the Church, and an ever-transforming Chinatown: "Cardinal O'Connor asked me to come down here for three months, on April Fool's Day. I'm not a priest of the archdiocese of New York, I'm a Maryknoll priest, the Catholic Foreign Missionary Society of America. So he knew me, said he heard we have a very difficult situation in Chinatown, we need someone who speaks Chinese, would you come down for three months? And here I am.

"Here I am because it's a rewarding, exciting place to be. I like the pastoral work. There's a whole new group of immigrants coming in, and so there's a whole different challenge. I was on my way to Cambodia, because that was one of the places that I took care of out of the central office. My previous experience was that I was a priest in Hong Kong for fifteen years. I was ordained in 1969 and was sent directly to Hong Kong. There I did mostly pastoral and school work in the resettlement states where Maryknoll has missions. And then I became the Superior for Hong Kong and Macau. And then China opened up. We went into China in '79 and '80; they were not ready for tourists or anything. And it was very exciting to visit all of the churches and the missions. And of

Rev. Raymond Nobiletti, M.M.

course Maryknoll, our society, was founded many, many years ago to go to China, so I had a lot of relationships with China and the Church, bringing priests over here to train them.

"I am a native New Yorker, born in Brooklyn, grew up in the Bronx and Long Island. When I decided to come down here my father said, 'What are you crazy? Go back to Hong Kong.' Because the city was really a mess then and so was Chinatown.

"I was here, I don't know how long, maybe a year, and there was a van that went through Baxter Street full of Filipino tourists in it. There was a gang street fight and they shot across the street and killed a woman in the van. I remember Chinatown emptied out for three weeks. There was tons of graffiti all over. There were some gangs on Pell Street and some other kids would walk down Pell and they'd get beat up. They'd come into the church and I was often going to the emergency room. And these were people we didn't even know. Then it changed, it really changed with the [Rudolph] Giuliani administration, law and order. A lot of these little dumpy coffee or dumpling shops that you knew weren't doing much business but there were gangs hanging out at them were closed. And so the whole tenor changed. Not that there's no crime in Chinatown. After that the new immigrants came and they have their own problems. You know when the *Golden Venture* [a ship bearing almost 300 illegal immigrants from China, which ran aground in Rockaway, Queens, in 1993] came, the police called us up because you know they were all speaking Fujianese and they had no Fujianese-trained police. And there really weren't that many Fujianese here either, this was early on. So they called us asking if we had any Fujianese speakers. Bottom line, they had about six or eight young people that they couldn't put in jail because they were underage. A number of these kids stayed here for those first couple of days. They were children, boys. One of them is getting married here in October in the church. It's been thirteen years. He's thirty now.

"The new immigrants have a lot of needs. My experience has been with the Cantonese, but they're really different people, a completely different language. So I went to Fuzhou twice.

"This is the largest Chinese Catholic congregation in the United States. The parish, because it was started in 1827, has territorial boundaries, but people come from all over the metropolitan area for services. If it was territorial it would probably be very poorly attended, because Chinatown is really changing. The families are moving out, even the families with kids. There are a lot of elderly people here. But

TRANSFIGURATION ROMAN CATHOLIC CHURCH & SCHOOL ㉙ 天容聖顯

on Sunday we have people coming from New Jersey, tons of people from Brooklyn, Connecticut, and Manhattan.

"Let me brag about this church. Most Catholic churches around the country are either all Cantonese speaking or all Mandarin speaking, or they're all some dialect. The Chinese are very prejudiced, like the Italian Americans or Sicilians, which is what I am. That's why they have all these churches. There was a Chinese priest here before, and a Chinese priest would naturally be aligned or associated with his people, Cantonese, Mandarin speaking, what have you. The advantage that I had being here is that I spoke Chinese, I knew the Chinese situation, but I was open to everybody. That's the American missionary thing, everybody who walks through the door gets served. Previously they'd direct some groups elsewhere, even the English speakers. Now we have a huge English-speaking congregation made up of Chinese Americans. The next generation.

"What I am proud about here is that the Cantonese really went out to the Mandarin and Fujianese speakers, helped the kids with language learning and schools. There is a whole network. And we have here now masses in English, Mandarin, Cantonese, and Fujianese all going at once. The parish tells me though, they say, 'You know, when you go and there's a Chinese pastor it's going to change.' I am the 'foreign ghost' that doesn't know any

better. So you get excused when things go wrong . . . it's an advantage. When I was in Hong Kong I was working with two kids, and if we did something that someone in the parish didn't like they'd [blame] one of those two kids. Me they didn't touch. They respect you for learning their language.

"This Easter—and almost every Easter it's the same number—we baptized forty-two adults. They studied for a year or more. And I have a great staff here, two sisters, one Chinese and one American. This year there were four priests, two from mainland China and a Jesuit, all trilingual. The parish now, the building and everything, is totally debt free and self supporting. We have three schools, the elementary school at the church, a kindergarten in Confucius Plaza, and a Chinese school here on weekends. They're all totally self supporting, with waiting lists, which the bishop likes very much. While most schools in this area are closing down, we need more space. And the kids excel in the archdiocese, they're one of the top if not the top, but that's not me, that's the principal.

"The building here began as a Dutch Lutheran church. They were English speaking however, because there was a whole group of the Dutch community wanted to have services in English, and learn English. So it was founded in 1801 as the English Lutheran Church Zion.

"Ten years later the minister and the whole congregation turned Episcopalian. So it became an Episcopalian or Anglican church. By that time the religion in Manhattan and the city was Episcopalian, as the area became less and less Dutch and more English. The church went on as an Episcopal church until 1853, when it was bought out by the archdiocese of New York to serve the thousands and thousands of Irish immigrants in the area. At that time this little church was the largest Catholic parish in the country—only because there were just a handful of Catholics in the rest of the country.

"This was the big immigration, so we had thousands of people packed into this church, which brings me to the story of Father Felix Varela.

"Father Varela was a Cuban priest in the 1800s, a philosopher and a seminary teacher, and he was so popular that he was elected as one of the two representatives from Cuba to the Spanish legislature. He wrote a lot about democracy. So he goes to Spain and he advocates two things: the abolition of slavery, and the separation of Cuba from Spain. Needless to say, he did not return to Cuba; they wouldn't let him go back. So he ends up in New York City and he rents St. Peter's on Barclay Street, which is the oldest Catholic parish, around the 1820s. He started two churches, one on Ann Street and one on John Street, all for Irish Catholics. He fought for them against the British; he fought for them in the school system, which they thought was too Protestant. He became known as the priest for the Irish. He was pastor here for twenty-three years. By the end of his time here he had given away all of his worldly possessions and became a saintly man. In 1996 when Pope John Paul II went to Cuba, which was unprecedented, I was invited. There were Felix Varela centers all over Cuba because he was like the Thomas Jefferson of Cuba—he wrote about freedom. And when the Holy Father left Cuba, the gift given to him at the airport by Fidel Castro were the works of Felix Varela, the pastor of this parish.

"Then the whole place turned Italian. And the Italian priests came in from Italy. And then it became Chinese. Maryknoll, my order, ran this place from 1949 to the seventies. They took responsibility for it because it was Chinese speaking, but then they gave it to the diocese.

"In many places on the Lower East Side you see synagogues that are now Pentecostal temples, but the Pentecostal temples now are being abandoned and they are turning into something else, because the church goes down to a cultural level. But this place has been going strong, nonstop. And the real test came with the Chinese because the Irish were naturally Catholic, the Italians were naturally Catholic, but the Chinese weren't. But Maryknoll, from the forties on, they went out and did conversions. That's the key to having kept it going. It's an interesting place. I went to New York University and I got like a masters on this place, and we called it a synecdoche. A synecdoche is a part of a whole, the city of New York being a whole, and even though it's just a part of a whole it has all the characteristics of the whole. The church is a mirror of the history of the city of New York." ○

寺廟 TEMPLES

佛教或道教的寺廟在中國城裡的歷史並不長

CHINATOWN DOES NOT HAVE A LONG HISTORY of Buddhist or Taoist temple life. The joss house pictured here at the beginning of the twentieth century was thought by tourists to be a place of worship, but in reality the main function was fortune telling and incense lighting.

Professor Joseph Lee often takes his students on a tour of the many large and small temples now operating in Chinatown: "An interesting thing about Chinese temples is that you can just go into one temple or another. There is no strict membership. It's also very much a traditional practice within the Chinese religious culture that the woman handles the religious affairs for the family. The men show up on certain days of public ritual."

Entering a temple, you can see the hierarchy of the altars. For example, a small Buddha altar may be set in the center as you enter, with a larger image of a deity in back. This is both convenient, as you can pray to Buddha and deities in one place, and be respectful to the beliefs that coexist. Most people in Chinatown tend to be some combination of Taoism, Confucianism, and Buddhism. Deities like Guan Kwong or Guan Yin, don't belong to the Buddhist, Confucian, or Taoist traditions, but these deities—as recognized by the emperor—joined the family of worship within the Chinese culture, much like saints.

"Wong Tai-Sin is understood as the deity for healthcare, so people who come to the Wong Tai-Sin temple (at 20 Bowery), many of them elderly, have a specific wish. If you come in the morning," suggests Dr. Lee, "after people have done their shopping, they will bring all their food and show it to the god, ask the god to bless it, then take it home and share it with their family. People come here for fortune telling, to pray for the health of the family and for celebrations. They understand religion in terms of pragmatic issues. It's not very intellectual, it's about seeing the result. If they don't see the result from one deity, they will move to another."

ABOVE: Dr. Joseph Lee, Associate Professor of History at Pace University. OPPOSITE: Joss house "altar," early twentieth century.

One social theory, Dr. Lee relates, is that the imperial state used ritual to expand into the local grassroots society to bring people together in southern China in the fifteenth or sixteenth centuries, and that the Taoist priest was one of these instruments. Taoist priests, who passed an exam and were licensed by the state, would traditionally travel around the Chinese countryside to conduct funerals and other religious practices according to the official texts. So when they would see some kind of shamanistic practice, they would condemn the shaman and then impose the official version on the local people.

Instead of putting up direct confrontation, the local people incorporated some of their popular religious elements into the Taoist temple. A good example of this is fortune telling—which is also seen incorporated into Buddhist temples around Chinatown. You can take a paper fortune here in exchange for a dollar donation. Professor Lee says that you can still see this in Canton and Fujian, as they were some of the last to be converted to Confucianism. Taoist priests also conducted ancestor worship; they believed that encouraging this practice would help the illiterate population internalize the idea of respect for the emperor. This ritual unity, along with a common written language, was key in keeping China united as an empire.

The Eastern States Temple at 64 Mott Street was started by a devout Buddhist practitioner, Annie Ying, and her husband, James Ying. The Yings immigrated here in the mid-fifties, and became successful owners of souvenir and tourist shops—first in Times Square, then on Mott Street, and later they had the first gift shop on top of the World Trade Center. When they arrived there weren't any Buddhist temples on the East Coast, so Annie simply set up a statue at the back of the store. Recognizing the need for it in the community, however, by the mid-sixties she decided to open a Buddhist temple in Chinatown. She brought masters and monks

ABOVE: Mahayana Temple Buddhist Association, 133 Canal Street. PREVIOUS PAGE: Main hall of worship.

from China to give teachings, and some of them stayed on and opened their own Buddhist temples here. This was just the beginning for the Ying family, as they later opened the Taoist temple on the Bowery, a full-size Mahayana Buddhist temple in South Cairo, New York, and in 1996 the largest temple in Chinatown, Mahayana, in a former theater. Famous in the community and beyond for their efforts, and now four generations strong, the family even oversees the China Pavilion at Disney World.

At fifteen feet high, Mahayana has one of the largest temple Buddha statues on the East Coast, seated in gilded splendor in the main hall. Dr. Lee instructs, "Come in and look at the face of the Buddha . . . does he look down or does he look away? In this way you get a sense of the power of the relationship between the deity and the worshipper."

As Molly Chen, a volunteer at the temple, puts it, "The temple is for Chinese people's spirits. To help people live better. People come here looking for peace." ○

As you enter Mahayana temple, the first area of worship is dedicated to Guan Yin, the Buddha of compassion. Originally this was a male figure, but Dr. Lee explains that over time the image became that of a woman, perhaps because of the large number of women in China who came to Guan Yin to pray to have a son and for the well-being of their family. Many of the sculptures and images in the entryway depict Guan Yin holding or near infants.

FROM TOP LEFT: **1.** This is the masters' room at Mahayana, where visiting monks wait before service. Lining the walls are photographs of the Ying family's altruistic endeavors outside the temple, including the Dr. Nelson Ying Science Competition for Orange County Orlando and the Barbara Ying Center for foreign students at the University of Central Florida. **2.** In alcoves in the main hall of Mahayana, pictures of the deceased are placed by relatives. Families give a donation, and the temple monks pray for the souls of the deceased. **3.** This publication is printed by the temple to teach people about Buddhism, and the different bodhisattvas are displayed and described in a simplified manner. **4.** On the second floor of the Mahayana temple is a lovely gift shop, plus the delightful and unexpected private collection of museum-quality Buddhist art and treasures owned by Dr. Ying. On these small tablets, you can write a prayer which can then be hung in the trees, for example outside of a temple. **5.** Small wooden books for sale, on which are written a sutra, or prayer. These are often placed in front of altars.

6. Main altar at Sung Tak Temple of New York, 15 Pike Street. 7 and 8. Puchao Temple, 20 Eldridge Street. Meaning "universal blessing," Puchao is a very popular deity in the Fujian area of China, appropriately, as the temple is located in the center of Little Fujian on Eldridge. On the altar from left to right you can see the Buddha of the past, the Buddha of the present, and the Buddha of the future. 9 and 10. The Guan Kwong Temple of America, Canal between Eldridge and Forsyth Street. This temple is dedicated to Guan Kwong, a general of the sixth or seventh century AD who was known to be very loyal to his master. He also had courage on the battlefield and is portrayed looking quite fierce. The Chinese Emperor probably made him a deity due to his loyalty, but, Dr. Lee says, when people worship Guan Kwong they are generally looking to draw from his courage and fierce qualities. 11. Another large temple, this one run by monks, Sung Tak is located in a former synagogue. 12. A laughing Buddha from the Mahayana collection. 13. Located on the north side of Canal between Eldridge and Forsyth, this is more of a traditional religious association, or shrine. The name on the exterior translates as "A paradise where you feel good, where you feel grateful, where you feel beneficent." Most of the time it's a kind of fortunetelling in these type of establishments, says Dr. Lee, almost like a counseling service with a religious connotation. 14. Secondary altars along the side at Sung Tak.

LOOKING BACK AND GIVING BACK

Jan Lee

沿
街
散
步

STROLL DOWN MOTT STREET and just after you've crossed Mosco, you'll come across an artful display of antiques and decorative objects in a sliver of a shop window. Jan Lee, the owner of Sinotique, is a second-generation Chinatown native, his grandfather having immigrated from Toisan province.

The family grew up on Mott Street, in the building that Sinotique occupies. The children all attended P.S. 23, then both of Jan's brother's, Timothy and Geoffrey, went to Brooklyn Tech—as their father, an aeronautics engineer, had done. But Jan, the youngest, followed in his sister Audrey's footsteps and attended the High School of Music and Art. This step, he says, set the basics for his aesthetic career, and he eventually graduated from Green Mountain College in Vermont with a degree in business management and a fine arts minor.

In 1992, at the age of just twenty-seven, Jan opened Sinotique. Three years later, after using local dealers exclusively and struggling with the margins, he went to buy in Asia. With this trip, his career changed. He was able to develop his eye, and a successful business in the design community followed.

In Chinatown, Jan is known for taking on problems as a community advocate. One of the toughest battles that the neighborhood has faced is parking, particularly since 9/11, when government employees from the courthouses began parking on the streets with no regard to the businesses they were disrupting. Beyond being economically difficult, as delivery trucks and visitors cannot park, it's dangerous when fire trucks can't get to their hydrants or access the building properly. The Catholic church has even had problems getting coffins over parked cars during funerals. Jan has taken the issue head-on, confronting the police, attending every community meeting or forum, galvanizing the shopkeepers—and he's gotten the attention of the government officials.

ABOVE: A hard-won immigration photo of Jan's grandfather. LEFT: Jan Lee at Sinotique, 19A Mott Street.

He was actually arrested for taking a photo of illegally parked cars. Protecting the community and lifestyle of Chinatown is a clear passion for Jan, who treasures the village-like atmosphere of the neighborhood.

Jan generously opens his family album to tell the story of his father Shung Lee's life in New York. Happily, Mr. Lee was an avid and very gifted photographer in his own right, as evidenced by the extensive and beautiful photographs in the collection, capturing a lifetime of memories for his family.

"There is a certain noble struggle that the Toisanese have as a history here in Chinatown," Jan explains. "My grandfather came over on a steamer clipper. It took him forty days to get here and he was deported twice. He jumped ship trying to come in: But the third time was the charm and he was sponsored legally. My grandmother was detained on Ellis Island for a year." Jan's family has a large altar to his grandfather in their house, which is a part of their Confucian upbringing. "There is a very deep root in my family, the tie to him and what he did to get here."

The family ran a laundry business in the late 1920s on the site of Jan's store. They were the only Chinese family living there in the beginning; the rest were Italian and Jewish. Jan's grandfather had the foresight to buy real estate in Chinatown when none of his contemporaries were interested in doing so.

When Jan's father graduated from P.S. 23 in 1934, he was the only Chinese American in his class; the rest were Italian and Jewish. In contrast, by the time Jan got there, there was just one Jewish kid, who was the principal's son. "My generation was the last where it was all just one dialect, Toisanese," says Jan, who notes the huge influx that came from Hong Kong after that. When he was a child, he remembers, "You'd go from house to house and have sleepovers and it was like your mother was cooking for you, because all the Toisanese cooked the same way." After visiting Hong Kong, Jan realized he had to learn to speak Chinese—meaning Cantonese.

Jan's mother's family was Indonesian Chinese, and they owned the largest rice mill on Lombok Island. The Japanese decimated everything during World War II. The women had to hide out in the forest, and made oil lamps from tuna fish cans. "My mother's schoolteacher was beheaded in front of the class, thankfully not in front of my mother." One of her classmates went into a permanent state of shock and never spoke again. "There was always a fear of rape, which is why the women had to run when they knew the Japanese were coming."

Following a childhood pasion for planes, Shung Lee trained at the Dallas Aviation School and Air College from 1937 to 1939, and at Centre

TOP: Jan's family's building on Mott Street. Underneath the street sign is the roof of the stand that Jan's grandfather built for his wife to sell preserves. BOTTOM: Jan's grandfather with his children and grandchildren.

College of Kentucky from 1943 to 1944, where he furthered his studies in what would become his life's work—aeronautical engineering. Mr. Lee was enlisted as a radio engineer and a gunner in the air force from July 1943 to January 1946. In 1948 Mr. Lee left to spend some time in Hong Kong after the early death of his first wife, who left him with an infant daughter, Jan's half-sister Valerie. The time away from New York was at the suggestion of his father, who was going back and forth doing business in Hong Kong, with the intention of relieving him of his grief, but also of finding him a wife. Through a mutual friend, Jan's parents met in China, where she was going to school, and hit it off. They lived there together for a year or so before returning to New York. In his free time, Shung Lee pursued his interest in fishing with his children that led him to buy a cabin in East Hampton in 1949. They bought a larger house near there in 1965.

As Jan's grandfather went back and forth to China, Jan's father and his sister Lonnie were the only two children born here in America. She and Shung Lee opened up a malt shop, Lonnie's, in their building in the 1960s. It had nothing to do with Chinese food, serving burgers, egg creams, lime rickeys, and pastries from Sutter's. "It was a well-known landmark," says Jan. "Italian kids grew up in it, a lot of Chinese kids grew up in it. And it was a niche market because a lot of Chinese kids wanted to have a hamburger, but you had to go out of the neighborhood to get one. So they really flourished for quite a few years. My whole family flipped hamburgers." Lonnie's closed in the early eighties.

When Jan's father was growing up, the family lawyer had a farm upstate in Duchess County, and he'd bring the whole Lee clan there for visits. "I guess it was imprinted in my father's head that he loved farms," laughs Jan. In 1980 they happened to notice an ad in the paper for a property upstate and promptly drove five hours to see it. Within a year, they'd found a farm to purchase in Whitehall, at the base of Lake Champlain. "We met incredible people up there. Our friends up there had no interest in coming to New York City.

"I was very fortunate; I have never taken for granted how fortunate I am and how fortunate my family is. Both my parents and my grandfather were very out-of-the-box. They were never afraid to be the only one in their town. When my family bought the house in East Hampton, there was not a single Chinese family living there." Shung Lee passed away in 2006, leaving a legacy that lives through his family, who speak of him with reverence and affection. "My father was very strong and extremely well spoken," and Jan recalls with a smile, "Growing up on the Lower East Side, he could talk his way out of anything."

TOP: As in many neighborhoods in Manhattan at the time, stickball was big when Shung Lee was a boy. Here he is in 1936, with his stickball team on the ramp to the Manhattan Bridge. BOTTOM: Strolling down the beach in Hong Kong.

TOP: 70 Mulberry, on the corner of Bayard, was formerly P.S. 23, the neighborhood elementary school. FAR LEFT: A fascination with planes began at a very young age for Shung Lee, seen here with a model plane in Columbus Park. LEFT: Shung Lee trained at the Dallas Aviation School and Air College from 1937 to 1939. Attending Centre College of Kentucky from 1943 to 1944, Shung Lee furthered his studies in what would become his life's work: aeronautical engineering. Growing up with an engineer as a father, Jan says he learned how to fix a lawn mower and work on cars. BOTTOM LEFT: Mr. Lee was enlisted as a radio engineer and a gunner in the air force from July 1943 to January 1946. "Toward the end of his life he lost the hearing in his right ear, because that was the one that had been closest to the engine," says Jan. BOTTOM RIGHT: The coffee shop in the 1960s.

SAM WONG

SAM WONG'S FAMILY HISTORY IN THE UNITED STATES reaches back many generations, to some of the first days of Chinese immigration. "My great-great-great-grandfather didn't come here for the railroad, didn't come here for the laundry business—he came here to open gambling businesses in San Francisco," Sam reveals. "At that time, when the men reached twenty they would go back to China, find a wife, and stay there two years. The wife would get pregnant. If it was a girl she'd stay [in China], but if it was a boy [the father] would come back when he reached age ten and bring him to the United States. That's how my great-great-great-grandfather came, and then when he grew older he did the same routine. So that's how it kept on going up until my grandfather, who was in San Francisco already."

With generations sending money back to China, Sam's family became very wealthy: "We had our own village, we had workers and servants." This was exactly the type of family that the Communists targeted when they took over, and his grandmother, mother (who was already married to his father), and younger uncle still remained in China. "When the Communists came over they took our village and tortured my grandmother," Sam explains. "They'd say 'You have money, now we want you to see how it feels to be poor.' The stories my grandmother told me . . ." Sam shakes his head. "One day they broke all the glass on the floor. She had to kneel on the floor for twenty-four hours—so that she would know how it felt to work on a farm, on your knees in the water. And they took a basket of snakes, 'Put your head in there!' Stuff like that."

There were very few options for families who wished to escape mainland China at the time, so Sam's family did the only thing they could. "My mother, my grandmother and my uncle swam to Hong Kong. Seven days. They had a piece of board [as a flotation device]. They started out with forty people and only seven survived. Most of them were eaten by sharks, or fell asleep and drifted off. They never really wanted to talk about it, but my grandmother wanted me to know before she died." Sam was born in 1956 in Hong Kong, soon after. "When I was eight my grandmother went to the market to buy food and ran into the lady, the person who had tortured her. So my father kinda put a hit man on her, but my grandmother said, 'You know, forget it, it's past. We're here right now. Leave her alone.'"

Sam's parents, reunited in Hong Kong, eventually set their sights on coming to America. "My mother's older brother was in the States, so he sponsored my mother, me, and my father in 1965. I came to Chinatown when I was nine years old, and I totally freaked out." Sam remembers, "In Hong Kong I lived a pretty good life because the money coming from the United States was a lot stronger. You know what I moved into? An apartment on Elizabeth and Spring, Dominican neighborhood, sixth floor, no elevator, cracked windows, all the paint was chipped. And the bathroom and the sink were set up in the middle of the living room. I said to my parents, 'Why are we here?' You see, in Hong Kong at that time, when you looked at movies you saw *The Sound of Music*, the American dream, snow, backyard . . . I hated it; I wanted to go home."

Sam started school at P.S. 130; he knew a little bit of English because he'd gone to Catholic school in Hong Kong, but not much. He recalls, "I remember the first time I went to the supermarket. I wanted to buy ice cream, but I bought the wrong thing. I bought cottage cheese—'cause it was the same container!"

Mr. and Mrs. Wong followed a typical immigrant path. His mother immediately took a job in a factory while his father worked in a restaurant, Sam says, "to pay back my uncle for the money he'd used to sponsor us, $5,000—that was a lot of money." Sam was an only child and a latch-key kid at age ten. "I was home by myself, and I learned how to cook. If I didn't cook I wouldn't survive. I would make dinner for them. They would come home at ten or eleven.

Fashion was very important. At one point in Chinatown all the gang members wore black-and-white jackets, all custom made. The inside lining would be white and the outside black. The higher rank you were, the more money you had and you'd have silver dragons embroidered on it.

"We'd hang out at Columbus Park a lot, and it became a territory. We had Mott Street, certain people got Bayard Street, certain people got Pell. And they were named Flying Dragons, the White Eagles, stuff like that. And at that time in Chinatown there were a lot of youth clubs, like Young Life, Horizons, and they all had parties. Always somehow those parties created problems, because there was only a handful of girls. All my best friends' wives," Sam laughs, "I went out with them then.

"It got a little more violent in the seventies. People started dying. If one gang member died, guaranteed next month another member died. It went on and on and on." Sam started to look for a way out. He remembers, "When I was seventeen my friend's father-in-law had an Asian vegetable company, like bok choy, snow peas. I helped out on weekends to ship things to Ohio. So one night I can't sleep. I thought, 'What am I doing here? I'm the lucky one; the unfortunate ones are in jail. What am I going to do, I can't do this forever.' I didn't want to be stuck in this stinking place where I had rats crawling over my arm."

In a moment of introspection, the first such moment of several that would punctuate his life, Sam had a vision that night. "Out of curiosity, I had noticed that the vegetables we were shipping cost $15 and the airfare was $85. So I thought, 'What if I took the vegetables to Ohio by truck and sold it to restaurants for $50 instead of $100?'" He talked to his friend's father and asked if he could take his accounts. Sam says he responded, "As long as you give me $15, I don't care what you do with it." So September 23, 1974, the day before Sam turned eighteen, he bought a Toyota Celica, packed his black-and-white TV, his underwear, a toothbrush, and his sleeping bag, and drove to Cleveland, Ohio.

He'd saved $500, so he checked into a hotel and paid $300 for the whole month. He then went over to the

"When that happens when you're ten years old, come to a new world, new language, new culture, you can start drifting off into the wrong crowd of people. And I did hang out in the gangs in Chinatown. You know why? Now you can see it has nothing to do with the kid, it's the parents. Somebody sponsors you and right away they have to go to work, forget about the children. The children had no choice [but to hang out in gangs] because they had no parents. Ten or twelve years old, we're hanging out on the street."

Sam remains in contact with some of his childhood friends and says, "Now we talk about it and think, what the hell were we doing? We'd stand out on the street for two hours! We'd stand out on any corner that had a stoop and talk about dreams. We wanted this or that car.

Cleveland telephone company and asked for all of their Yellow Pages. He remembers, "I wrote down all of the Asian restaurants on a piece of paper. Got a map, and put thumbtacks where the addresses were. Then I called all of them. I said, 'My name is Sam, I'm from New York and I'm in Cleveland now. If I got bok choy in your refrigerator for $50 would you buy it from me?' One guy said 'I'd kiss your feet.' So I picked up the orders, and I took a Greyhound bus back [to New York] for $7. Then I rented a U-Haul, loaded up the bok choy and brought it there.

"That's how the whole thing started. It got bigger and bigger. By age twenty-two I had seven tractor-trailers. I made so much money. I threw it on the bed and jumped on it! *Lassie* was popular, so I bought a collie. I bought a six-bedroom house, with a swimming pool, four-car garage—at twenty-two years old! At that moment, all my American dreams came true."

Sam ran his business until he was twenty-seven. He explains, "I had a nervous breakdown, I was too young. I couldn't handle all the stress, and I got an ulcer. The doctors said you've got to stop working." So Sam returned to Chinatown from Ohio, married briefly, and set about starting over. At that time Sam's father owned a restaurant in Chinatown, the first dim sum restaurant at 9 Pell Street. "But don't forget," Sam says, "my father carried the family thing down. He owned about three or four gambling houses, and was involved with the tong on Pell Street. My family was always connected, we had to be. That's why I felt like I was stuck in a circle. The people I went to school with don't want to leave Chinatown and they don't speak English to this day. They live here, they work here. They never venture into Wall Street, they never go over the Brooklyn Bridge."

When Sam returned to New York, his father urged him to join the family business, but Sam searched for other opportunities. "I came up with a crazy idea. A good friend of mine I grew up with was into the seafood business so I got involved with him. I started selling frozen seafood, but the clients I picked up were different.

I didn't pick them up in Chinatown, I went up to the Russian Tea Room, the '21' Club, the River Café, most of the high-end Japanese restaurants. I didn't want to stay in Chinatown."

Sam worked two hours a day, taking phone orders, and eventually he says, "ended up hanging out with all of these trust-fund babies." The first one he met was the son of a top restaurant owner. "We'd go out spending $3,000 average a night, drinking Cristal, caviar, coke, pot. But don't forget for them to do that every night is fine, I made money but I was earning it. But I had to hang out with them to get all those accounts. At that time I lived on Sixty-fourth between Second and First. Every Friday, Saturday we hung out at the clubs like the Palladium. After the clubs closed we'd hang out at the after-hours clubs. We'd come out like vampires at four.

"I got lost," says Sam. One day he went home on a Thursday and crawled into bed. The next thing he knew, his mother, who came once a week to clean and check up on him, woke him and he responded, "What, it's Friday?" And she said, "No, it's Monday." Sam had slept for four days. "I was so burned," remembers Sam. It was then that Sam would have a second moment of clarity. "I guess I feel lucky. I had a vision, I had time to wake up. I packed my stuff again and went to Canada where I didn't know anybody, no one knew who I was, and there were no drugs around."

Sam spent two months hanging out, sightseeing, and driving all over Canada until his money ran out. Sam recalls, "I had two dollars in my pocket and a full tank of gas. I couldn't pay for tolls, so I got out a map and took Route 2 and side roads from Canada." Filled with wonder, Sam recalls, "It's gorgeous, did you know we have castles in the U.S., up near Rochester? You feel like you're in Ireland, all farmland, sheep crossing the road. It was the best time of my life. And then I stopped in this small town in Pennsylvania. I went in there to buy a soda and go to the bathroom, and this town was all Eurasian! I asked, are you half Chinese, they said yes. There was a Chinese museum and everything. So I spoke to the owner of this coffee shop and basically during the building of the railroad a group of Chinese cut out—you know they were basically slaves—and migrated to that town."

The entire trip Sam had been asking himself, "What did I do wrong? Why did my marriage go wrong, the American dream? I had worked hard, provided for my family. I had all of that, but I didn't know how to balance it." But the last night, in Niagara Falls, he says he stopped asking those questions and realized he needed to go back to New York and, he says, "figure out what I *didn't* want from life, or I would never know what I wanted. So I got rid of all the friends I didn't want to hang out with, cut out all of my bad habits, and that was it."

Sam returned to New York and came up with the idea to buy Walter's, a deli that had been in Chinatown on Mulberry Street since he was a kid. It was the place everybody went, Sam says, when they were "sick of eating won ton noodles," so they'd go get a turkey sandwich. It was the only place in the whole area for that, he says. But Walter wouldn't sell, so Sam ended up opening Sam's Deli at 30 Mulberry Street—which still stands today (although Sam has since sold it).

Life as a deli owner in Chinatown had its surprises. Sam recalls, "I kept thinking my target would be the American-born Chinese, but I didn't realize I'd get the Department of Motor Vehicles, the court, Health Department—they were sick of Chinese food, too, and wanted a sandwich! Next thing I know I'm doing 400 sandwiches an hour. The line was all the way down the block."

He ran Sam's for ten years, but eventually got bored. In a chance meeting on Henry Street in Brooklyn, Sam ended up buying a Chinese restaurant from a friend of his, partnering with an old friend named George Donohue. The restaurant was Cinnamon Tree at 114 Henry Street. Sam describes, "We went in there and changed the whole concept, put in a baby grand piano, had jazz every night." The neighborhood responded well and when an opportunity came up in the St. George Hotel, the pair was approached to repeat their "magic" there. So Sam came up with another concept: upscale diner food. It was casual—anybody could walk in and get something to eat, at a great quality and price. They called it Sage (for Sam and George).

Over the course of several years, Sam pulled out of Sage and grew tired of Cinnamon Tree. He took the opportunity to open a Thai restaurant with a young chef named Chris Chung. Sam went about creating a mood for the space while Chris developed the menu. At a shop on Mercer Street he found beautiful old pictures of Asia in a book, had them shot and blown up in sepia for the walls. Thai Grill was a hit. They never skimped on ingredients, using fresh lime leaves, for example. Chris was there for two years and then left to open Celadon, but Sam continued running it for ten years. "I was working day and night, then I found out I had cancer. When the doctor told me that I said whoa, I took a step back, went in three days a week."

Toward the end of his treatments, in 2001, Sam and Chris opened Tiger Blossom on Bleecker and the Bowery. Another success, they were booked solid from July to January 15. "We were open for four months, then September 11 came, and it was all over," says Sam. "No matter how good you are in the restaurant business, without luck on your side it won't work."

A few years later, in July 2005, Sam and Chris opened Little Bistro, a small, forty-seat location in Cobble Hill, Brooklyn, serving New American food. The restaurant was another hit with the neighborhood and the press.

In September 2005, Sam's cancer came back. During treatments, he was exhausted and his lease came up at Thai Grill, "so I gave the landlord the key and walked away." Sam and Chris still have Little Bistro, and have gone on to open Almond Flower in Chinatown, which shares a similar menu.

Sam had been approached by three partners from Chinatown to open Almond Flower; one who owns the biggest real estate company, one the biggest ad agency, and another the largest newspaper. Opening a restaurant or shop in Chinatown can be completely debilitating financially, as in most cases you have to pay fixture fees

or key money to the landlord in order to get the lease. It's essentially a nonrefundable deposit that can be as much as $200,000. In the case of Almond Flower someone defaulted on rent and the partners decided to use the space, offering Sam a partnership and assuring him, as he felt he had no concept of how to market to the community, that they would handle that aspect. Sam then approached Chris and said, "Hey, Chris, we're Asian, let's go back to Chinatown and make our name in Chinatown." Sam laughs, "In the beginning, we kinda looked at each other . . . and said wait, we totally forgot who we are. We've only been serving the American market. So we said let's go back and give them real, good American food."

In the way Sam describes his return to the neighborhood, there is the feeling he has come full circle, entering a world that has become foreign to him, as new immigrants have arrived from mainland China. "When I came back to Chinatown I rented new Chinese films to learn the new slang," he says, "because I need to know it when the workers talk to me—and I bought the latest music from Hong Kong."

The experience has given Sam another perspective on his own rapidly changing community. "When we opened, I met so many high-powered Chinese people. I couldn't believe they exist because I was never involved in this world, in my own community. And now I see people make it here, it's unbelievable."

Sam was recently asked to come to Beijing to work on restaurant openings and concepts in preparation for the Beijing Olympics. It's a huge honor, but a decision that rattled him a bit. He explains somberly, "When my grandmother, who had been tortured, was dying she said, 'Please promise me you won't go back to mainland China.'"

It's another chapter in Sam's eventful, ever-evolving life and one can imagine, perhaps another circle to close, this time for the legacy of his family.

(For more Sam and Chris's opening of Almond Flower, see page 117.)

JAMI GONG

AS A LICENSED CHINATOWN TOUR GUIDE, former president of the New York chapter of the Organization of Chinese Americans, a one-time Olympic torchbearer, and creator of Chinatownnyc.com, Jami Gong takes his community seriously, while bringing to it what he feels it needs, such as laughter. In December 2002, when the community was still feeling the difficult economic aftermath of September 11, the budding comedian started his TakeOut Comedy performances in Chinatown. This led to sold-out monthly shows and the first national Asian American comedy competition in 2004. From there they toured the country and ultimately performed in Hong Kong, where Jami has now opened Hong Kong's first-ever comedy club and comedy school, with hopes to expand into Shanghai and Beijing, to "bring more laughter into the area" and eventually create the Chinese version of *Last Comic Standing*. "The last five years have changed my life," says Jami. "I met people from all over the world."

Jami's story begins with his father, born and raised in a village in Guangzhou, the Toisan area. "In 1995 he brought me and my brother there," Jami remembers. "It was six hours one way from Guangzhou to the village. At that time the roads were pretty bad, so it was a torturous cab ride. He made my brother and I wear long pants because he was so proud to bring his two sons back to the village. It was one of the turning points of my life when I saw all the beggars on the streets. I thought, wow, I could have been one of them. When I came back to the U.S. I kissed the ground I walked on."

Jami's mother was born and raised in Hong Kong, where she became a schoolteacher, then met and married his father. Their first son was born in 1966. "After the racial quotas were lifted in 1965, a lot more people started to come to the U.S., especially from that area," explains

Jami. "So they came here in 1967." Jami's older sister was born in 1968, he was born in 1969 and the Gongs had three more children, with the youngest son being born in 1976.

"My father got into his acupuncture business while my mother took care of us and became a seamstress. She gave up teaching. That was big in the eighties, all my friends' mothers worked in the garment district. Mom would work from nine and come home and cook dinner at seven thirty. Looking back now I can see how hard my mom worked for all of us. She was working for pennies. We'd help her do draperies at home, we thought it was fun back then, and we knew she was getting paid fifty cents for whatever shirt she was making. She was working six days a week. I appreciate everything my family did. I was born and raised on Essex Street, then to 96 East Broadway, then Madison Street, where we've lived for over thirty years.

"Just like any Chinese parent, [my father will] tell you stories about how much they suffered during the Cultural Revolution. 'We would walk twenty miles to go to school,' he'd say, and each year it would get longer and longer," Jami jokes, "and he would tell us how easy we have it over here. They emphasized studying hard, like many Chinese parents, and all six of us went to Stuyvesant High School," one of the top public high schools in the country.

Jami's parents divorced in 1983, around the same time as his father's parents died. His grandfather had been a successful businessman who spoke perfect Spanish. "My father's mother did not like coming to the U.S. She was always very stern. I found out recently that she had been born into an affluent family and coming here she experienced a lower class, which explains some of the way she acted back then. My grandfather loved her to death, and she died just a couple of years after him."

Jami's mother's family never came to the United States, but his inspiration to create TakeOut Comedy in Chinatown came to him on a flight to Hong Kong to see his dying grandmother. Upon arrival he learned she had passed away during his flight. He believes this inspiration was her gift to him. "That was when I vowed to her that I needed to go back [to Hong Kong] to do comedy. She really devoted everything to us. The only regret that we have is that when her health deteriorated we didn't bring her over here to take care of her. But she is here in another way.

"My father wanted me to become an acupuncturist. I wish I had been more disciplined, and now looking back I wish I had stayed in Chinese school, taken kung fu classes. I was a wild kid. I am taking Mandarin classes right now and it's brutal!" Jami jokes about Asian parents all wanting their children to become doctors, with his parents being no exception. Jami's brother, who works in insurance, has a PhD in animal behavior; one sister is an Ob-Gyn; one was a Fulbright Scholar, another sister went to Yale and is now at Google; and the youngest is a teacher here in Chinatown. There are eight grandchildren thus far. "Not too shabby, huh?" asks Jami, shaking his head and smiling. "For my mom it's still not enough."

Running the comedy club and stand-up school in Hong Kong, Jami hopes to discover the "Hong Kong Jerry Seinfeld," relating that he wants to launch careers and "pass the torch." These days he says, "I don't yearn to be on the *Tonight Show*, as other comics do. I feel most productive being a producer and club owner." He loves inspiring people, giving speeches at colleges, and entertains the idea of becoming a motivational speaker one day. "I have always been a risk taker, and I don't do things for the money, I do things for the fun of it. Doing comedy is my calling," Jami asserts. "For me, going back to Hong Kong to do comedy, I have come full circle." **(For more on Jami's father see page 168. To see the latest on TakeOut Comedy go to www.TakeOutComedy.com)**

JAN HE

JAN HE IS A PASSIONATE COMMUNITY LEADER who has been recognized by the YMCA with a Reaching for the Stars nomination, and, having been nominated by her company, was named one of the Outstanding 50 Asian Americans in Business.

The first person in her family to come to the United States was her father's eldest brother, who was sent as a student by the Chinese government, on scholarship. But by the time he had finished his studies, the government had changed hands in China, so he decided to stay and ended up running a restaurant vegetable supply business (he was known as the King of Bean Sprouts) and a noodle shop on the Bowery. He then applied for his brother, Jan's father, and his family to come to the United States from Canton in the early eighties. Although Jan's father was a successful chemical engineer in China, he and her mother wanted their daughters to have a better life with more opportunity. Upon entering the United States they eventually went into the garment manufacturing

business. "My father stayed in the factory almost twenty-four hours a day, because he had to be there first to open early and close late. They worked very hard. I feel so happy for my father today," says Jan, "because he really enjoys his retirement, he travels and exercises."

Jan went to high school here and then college on financial aid. She says, "I am now in the financial consulting business because I feel that is a way that I can not only build a career for myself but help the community. After all, my job is to help build a better financial life for my clients." Jan has spent sixteen years in the business, and has more than 4,000 clients.

Originally she wanted to become a teacher and a social worker. She always volunteered in high school. "When I came here at sixteen I didn't speak English, but I was welcomed and helped. And by helping other people I learned from them." Jan was on the board of the Chinatown YMCA for eight years, with the goal of building a 40,000-square-foot community center on Houston Street, between the Bowery and Chrystie Street—which opened in 2006. "They never had a community center in this neighborhood," Jan emphasizes, "so this was a great challenge." Her dedication to the organization runs deep. "Two days after I arrived [in the U.S.] my father registered me in YMCA summer camp. We had to pay $150—that was a lot of money at that time. I still feel grateful toward this organization because they took me in, they gave me a lot of encouragement."

Jan cofounded the USA Chinese Women's Federation in 2000, an organization—now 200-strong—dedicated to gathering successful businesswomen together to nurture friendships and help the community. One of their first projects was to help recruit Asian foster families, as there hadn't been any—which was a "double impact for the children," as Jan puts it, for Asian orphans being placed into non-Chinese-speaking foster homes. "We're using our women's power to add something nice to the system," says Jan. They helped beautify the Allen Street mall, and helped work toward the changing of the name to Avenue of the Immigrants. Other accomplishments by the group include raising funds for and building a school for the deaf and disabled in Inner Mongolia, and hosting a monthly breakfast with sixty senior citizens from the community, to give them information on topics such as health issues. They were also invited to the International Women's Conference in Beijing, where they met similarly minded women from all over the world.

"The more I get to know my community, the more I know what they need," says Jan. So in 2005 she founded Asian Americans for New York.

She wants to be "a resource for the community because everybody is part of the mainstream in New York, but they have to participate. They have to vote. And then our voices will be heard if they are active bodies in the political system." She hosts gatherings so that elected officials can meet community leaders in an open format, and she was the Asian adviser on the mayor's campaign. Remarkably, Jan speaks Cantonese and Mandarin fluently and understands many dialects. Her chosen role as a bridge to the world beyond Chinatown is pivotal, and in some ways a more modern and connected solution to the roles associations have always played in the neighborhood. She explains that her goal is to "motivate people to become a part of the system and also help Asians build a better New York. My job gives me access to the community, so I want to utilize this opportunity to help the community."

TONY LIU

TONY LIU WAS BORN IN GUANGZHOU IN 1956, and he vividly recalls his childhood in China. With the food supply being scarce, his family used food stamps, and he would watch his father divide a bag of rice very precisely using a scale, to ensure portions for all the family members. He remembers one time sitting across the table from his father, watching him eat. His father looked up, and upon seeing his hungry son, stuck the last spoonful into his son's mouth. But what dominates are fond memories of his rural childhood, of falling asleep in his mother's lap on their stoop; the longan and lychee trees; the small shrimp in the pond across the street; colorful orange, red, green, and blue crabs that would appear in the brackish water at low tide; sailing paper boats and biting on dark purple sugarcane, so juicy and sweet, with his gaggle of neighborhood friends.

Seeking a better opportunity, his father eventually moved the family to Hong Kong and got work on a merchant ship where he would spend two or three months at sea but have better pay. An uncle in the United States petitioned to bring the family over in 1962. It took seven years, but by 1969 Tony, his parents, and his two younger sisters had finally arrived.

Tony's uncle was a part owner of a restaurant, his father worked

Tony Liu at his Bowery office. Behind him, alongside numerous commendations from MetLife, are posters of events that he has helped organize or sponsor in Chinatown, through his neighborhood magazine, *Focus New York*.

there, and after school Tony would go there to work as a dishwasher, as a good gesture. He remembers, "Pan-fried butterflied shrimp were most popular. I knew, as I washed the dishes—they sold like crazy!" As he began ninth grade he was working so much that his grades started to go down. "My father said shape up or ship out!" So he quit his job and made the honors program. Tony went on to attend Westinghouse High School, which was a tech-focused all-boys school, and then studied electronic engineering at New York City Community College. After graduation he started working on electronic prototypes at a company in New Jersey. "I sat there and said there has got to be a better way. I hate staying indoors." So he eventually got a job in sales for MetLife in 1985 and has been there ever since.

Today he also runs a public relations agency as well as *Focus New York* magazine, promoting Chinatown. "I want to promote the Chinese culture because of what happened to me in junior high. I couldn't speak English and was called Ching Ching Charlie Wong . . . I am a peaceful guy. You respect me in a measurement of one foot, and I will respect you back in a measurement of a yard. I do my part and I would like everybody to do that. For instance, [if I see someone] throwing orange peels on the street, I will start a casual conversation, then say 'Be careful what kind of example you are setting for yourself.'

"My kids feel proud to be Chinese. At the beginning [my daughter] would ask, 'How come you say Chinese this and Chinese that?' So I taught her no matter how you mingle you always look Chinese. Sometimes you get respect, sometimes disrespect, but you have to go deeper than that. What kind of person are you? I want people to know about the Chinese guy that lives next door. We're not all that different."

Tony started *Focus New York* in 2004 to help visitors familiarize themselves with Chinatown and thus help support the neighborhood economy. You can find the free issues, supported by local advertisers, in shops and restaurants around the neighborhood. Through his PR company, Toro Associates, he works with tour companies, and promotes food and walking tours, setting up entertainment such as traditional music or lion dance performances when requested. He is also involved in promoting the Dragon Boat Race each year, Taste of Chinatown, and the new annual Focus New York Ping Pong Tournament, which attracted a former Olympic player, Atanda Musa, from China in 2006.

Tony sees himself as able to communicate with both the older Chinese community and the younger generation of ABCs (American-born Chinese). "I am old enough to relate to the older community but young at heart." This puts him in a bit of a referee role as the community makes decisions about its future, he says, but he prefers that to the alternative of no communication, explaining, "If they butt heads that's good, that's community."

WELLINGTON CHEN

THE SON OF A NURSE WHO BROUGHT HIM and his younger brother to this country from Hong Kong via Brazil in 1970, Wellington Chen is now the executive director of the Chinatown Partnership Local Development Corporation, a nonprofit organization formed to support the future of the Chinatown community post-9/11.

Wellington attended City College, where he majored in architecture. "I worked my way up in small firms and medium firms, then in I. M. Pei's office for several years." He also spent thirteen years on the local Community Board in Flushing, working to turn around the decline of the community that began in the seventies. Flushing will have $4 billion flowing in in the next five years. "Everything comes with a price, though," Wellington says. "Schools and parks need public involvement. I was blessed because I have worked with designers, I have worked with communities and developers because of my architecture background, and these multiple perspectives become valuable and help me see through other people's lenses."

When asked why he joined the Chinatown Partnership, Wellington explains, "What intrigued me was the question, 'What should be the

twenty-first-century Chinatown?' We need to engage the outside, we can no longer hunker down and protect ourselves with all the associations. September 11 proved that we cannot exist in isolation, that we are heavily dependent on the outside community, whether it's for visitors, tourists, trade, people coming to eat. We need to engage the Lower East Side, Little Italy, the World Financial Center."

The Chinatown Partnership started as a community workshop. "It is a credit to the community that they see something has to be done," says Wellington. Most of the funding is targeted to clean the streets of Chinatown, based on the results of a survey by the Rebuild Chinatown Initiative, but there is still some left for other initiatives that must be carefully considered. "Our funding is generous but it is also limited in time. Sooner or later I turn back into a pumpkin," explains Wellington, "so I ask, 'What can I realistically accomplish?' I have a few years, after which the community must put forth matching funds.

"We are looking for sustainability, which is the hardest thing. That portion of it requires a great deal of strategic thinking. We are examining how best to leverage this precious gift to make it a long-term benefit for this community," explains Wellington. "Just like our forefathers laid down the railroad tracks and unified this country, that infrastructure is the investment."

Wellington's personal ancestry includes a grandfather who was a school principal who spoke up against the warlords and was killed, in a classic ambush assassination, with seven bullets. "My perspective is that of Buzz Aldrin, who says that we as humans should go back to the moon more often to look back at this little oasis called Earth. There are no boundaries, it's mostly water, we have very little precious land. There is only a certain amount of space for us to get together and celebrate. And this is what we need to do for Chinatown. The scarcity of availability of opportunity for immigrants to thrive is going to be a challenge for this organization."

Wellington reflects, "My father was the captain of a freighter. In 1961 there was a typhoon at 2 AM in the Indian Ocean. And a survivor saw my father jump off the propeller. He stayed with the ship, did his duty as the last one off, and a British warship picked up his body . . . People ask why I want to get involved in the community, and it's because of parents like that, they did their duty. My mother, all her life as well, was caring and helping others. It's a long way home, a long odyssey."

WILLIAM CHIU

IN ADDITION TO WORKING FOR NEW YORK LIFE INSURANCE
for over thirty years, William Chiu is chairman of the American Fujian
Association of Commerce and Industry, and says he helps by doing
whatever his people in his community don't have time to do. "I am there
for them," he says.

After 9/11 William was an advisory committee member of the Lower
Manhattan Development Corporation for four years. He would arrange
lion dances for the community, to draw people and business to the
neighborhood, sometimes attracting over 1,000 people. He himself was
trained in Hong Kong by a third generation (from the original master)
in Choy Lay Fut (Chai Li Fu) style of lion dancing. He met the master
after falling while running at age seven. "I was a very naughty boy," he
says, and they took him to his master, who promptly stopped the bleeding
with an herb. There is a soft side and a hard side to lion dancing, he
explains—it is both an art and a form of self-defense.

The Fujianese have been the fastest growing group of Chinese to
come to the United States over the last couple of decades. Speaking
of the neighborhood, he says, "Thirty years ago East Broadway was a
slum; now it's Fifth Avenue, and people don't want to leave." Although
he believes the community, particularly families, should probably move
somewhere else in the city, he has taken on real estate developers on the
community's behalf—which can be difficult, as some of the development
money coming in is drug-related. "Am I afraid? Yeah, I am afraid,
that's why I buy more insurance to cover myself," William jokes, "but
if everybody is afraid to talk about it then no one will talk about it, and
especially after 9/11 the economy here has been so bad."

When asked what he thinks is the biggest challenge for this
community, he responds, "I think they should stop checking people's IDs
on the streets in Chinatown. Without the new immigrants the economy

TOP: William Chiu at work at 11 East Broadway.
ABOVE: Mr. Chiu surveys a view of East Broadway.

would go down the drain . . . If they arrest people on the streets then they cannot come to Chinatown and shop."

William's association, which he formed in 1992, was called by the federal Immigration and Naturalization Service and police to claim the bodies during the tragic *Golden Venture* event. They were able to find four families, and the remaining six are now buried in New Jersey. The Ng Fook Funeral House donated the money for the burials. "It was very sad," William remembers. He and a head of another organization went to the beach to do a Buddhist ceremony for them, he explains, "for the people to go in peace. And we had a whole troop of police try to stop us. And there were only two people coming! Surprisingly we made the world news. And there was a memorial for the people in Flushing, the space was donated, by Amy Chan of Ng Fook. She is a really good lady and helps the community a lot."

William came from Hong Kong but his family originally hails from Fuzhou. Following back thirty-four generations, they are descendants of the emperor of the Sung Dynasty. He found this out when his grandmother passed away and he took her remains back to the temple in their village in Fuzhou. His mother had never talked about their family roots. "We were so poor, we had to work hard for a living, so it didn't matter." They came to the United States with nine family members in 1971. His father was a chef who had been trained in Shanghai and dreamed of immigrating. William remembers, "When he got here and tasted the food he was shocked. He said, 'Oh my gosh! This is Chinese food?'—the chow mein and chop suey being far from authentic fare. They opened a take-out restaurant near Stonybrook, Long Island, called Uncle Chao's Kitchen. Sadly, his father realized his dream of opening the restaurant here, but passed away within six months.

When the Grand Street subway station was closed due to construction on the Manhattan Bridge, William read the plans, and they claimed the station would be closed for eight years. "I went to a public hearing on the project and asked, 'Why do you really need eight years?' And the engineer from the project came out and I asked him, 'Are you really using three shifts to finish the job, or just one shift?' He said, 'I don't know.' And I said, 'Any engineer who has a project like this knows how many shifts they have. How come you don't know? That's baloney!' People applauded. And you know what happened? Two weeks later the engineer was locked up by the government. The job is done and he's still in jail. The station was reopened in less than three years." ○

THE RICE BOWL
CHINATOWN, NEW YORK.

PORT ARTHUR RESTAURANT, 7-9 Mott Street, New York

Ping Ping

Would you like to have a real Chinese Meal?

SOFT NOODLE
CHOW MEIN
CANTON
ROAST PORK
EGG ROLL
SWEET & SOUR FISH

1 2 3 4 9 10 11 12

Repasts: Then & Now

FROM TOP LEFT: 1. The stylish Rice Bowl was located on Mott Street. **2.** Ping restaurant on Mott Street. **3.** Boiling "Chinese tamales" at May May. **4.** A postcard sent from a Port Arthur Restaurant customer. **5.** The façade of Wo Hop on Mott. **6.** A Port Arthur menu cover depicts Chu Gow, the owner. **7.** Ping restaurant's main dining room **8.** Lou's Chinese American Cuisine's décor gave a newer look to Bayard Street. **9.** Glistening roasted meats at Hsin Wong. **10.** At the counter at Chatham Square. **11.** Most likely seeking to appeal to a wide audience, Yat Bun Sing advertised favorite Chinese-American dishes such as egg foo young and chow mein along with authentic staples like the exotic shark fins and roast duck—all while emphasizing the affordability of the Chinatown restaurant experience, an expectation that locals and visitors share to this day. **12.** Pictured here is the elaborate interior of a restaurant on Doyers Street circa 1905. To appeal to a broader audience, top, upscale Chinatown restaurants were often decked out in over-the-top chinoiserie, mixing different dynasties and extravagant furniture. Waiters wore tuxedos, and savvy proprietors struck a balance between the discovery of Chinese food and the familiar. **13.** Soup dumplings at Shanghai Café. **14.** The façade of Nom Wah Tea Parlor on Doyers Street. **15.** Restaurateur Spencer Chan. **16.** The interior of Mei Lai Wah, 64 Bayard Street.

Clay pot rice casseroles in the kitchen at Yummy Noodle, 48 Bowery.

六十八

樓 順 旅

PORT ARTHUR
RESTAURANT

7-9 MOTT STREET

New York City

Telephone: WOrth 2-5890

CHOP SUEY DAYS

饕客天

現今在美國中國餐館的數量幾乎是麥當勞的三倍

Table D'Hote Dinners

No. 1	No. 2
$1.00 DINNER	$1.50 DINNER
Chicken Mushroom Soup	Chicken Mushroom Soup
Port Arthur Almond Chicken	Chicken, Sliced, Fried with Mushrooms and Vegetables
Chicken Chow Mein	Mushroom Omelette
Rice	Roast Chicken (Canton Style)
Dessert:	Dessert:
Golden Limes Pineapple Almond Cake	Golden Limes Pineapple Almond Cake
Oolong Tea	Chinese Li-Chee Nuts
	Suey Sinn Tea

No. 3	No. 4
$2.00 DINNER	$2.50 DINNER
Celery Olives	Celery Olives
Chicken Bird's Nest Soup	Chicken Bird's Nest Soup
Almond Chicken	Pineapple Shrimp
Omelette a la Port Arthur	Almond Chicken Chow Mein
Duck, Sliced, with Bamboo Sprouts and Vegetables	Peking Roast Chicken
Dessert:	Dessert:
Golden Limes Pineapple Almond Cake	Golden Limes Pineapple Almond Cake
Chinese Li-Chee Nuts Ice Cream	Chinese Li-Chee Nuts Ice Cream
Loong Jan Tea	Woo Mee Tea

(12)

TOP: Expensive Bird's Nest Soup appears on a table d'hote menu. Each of the menus were served with a different tea—a far cry from the standard teapot of Pu-erh offered at many Chinatown restaurants today.
LEFT: A later Port Arthur menu cover.

TODAY THERE ARE ALMOST THREE TIMES AS MANY CHINESE restaurants in America as there are McDonald's. This astounding fact illustrates just how engrained in the fabric of American life the Chinese restaurant has become. The 150-year journey that Chinese Americans have made through the entrepreneurial endeavor of restaurant owner-ship has become the subject, in recent years, of articles and academic papers and an excellent exhibit by the Museum of Chinese in the Americas entitled "Have You Eaten Yet?" Trying to grasp the impact that the restaurant business has had on American culture, as well as the significant role it has played in the personal journeys of numerous immigrants to this day, is a fascinating and multilayered process that follows history and trends, chronicling the challenges and advances of the Chinese community. As I interviewed the people profiled in this book, nearly every person, regardless of their profession, had a link to the industry either directly or through their families.

Chinese food in America made its first significant debut in the "chow chow" restaurants of the mid-nineteenth century in San Francisco, catering to Cantonese workers. These basic-style establishments were not far from the type of places that could be found by the late nineteenth century in New York's Chinatown in the form of chop suey houses located on second or third floors of the congested neighborhood. Beyond the single men, locals, and laundry workers that the restaurants served, non-Chinese thrill seekers first sought out these establishments, for both the unusual foods and the danger of visiting the neighborhood, maligned in the press for its shady characters and opium dens. Restaurant owners eventually created more upscale restaurants that could accommodate family banquets and the growing tourist trade. This transformed the economy of the neighborhood, as food suppliers and tourist gift shops followed. Some

Port Arthur Restaurant (seen here in 1912) was one of the most famous Chinatown restaurants.

PORT ARTHUR

CHINESE RESTAURANT

NEW YEARS, CHINATOWN

of the most famous of the bigger restaurants were Port Arthur, The Oriental, and Chinese Delmonico's.

Coinciding with the end of the Exclusion Act, the 1940s ushered in the "nightclub era," and Chinatown became an entertainment hub for music, food, and gambling. It was at this time that diners began to see egg rolls, sweet-and-sour pork, and fried rice introduced. In the fifties and sixties, Chinese food began to go more downmarket. Fading away were the intricate interiors and glamorous destination dining, as the restaurants standardized with dishes designed for the American palate, ushering in the era of paper menus with instructions on how to use chopsticks. Dishes that became part of the American-Chinese repertoire included mu shu pork and kung pao chicken.

With President Richard Nixon's opening up of China in the 1970s came a renewed interest in more "authentic" Chinese food. And from 1965, as immigrants were allowed into the country in higher numbers, the market grew for more regional fare, and Chinese restaurants began once again to cater to the Chinese community as well as the non-Chinese.

SPENCER CHAN

AFTER LEAVING HONG KONG and arriving in the United States in 1976, Spencer Chan began working in the restaurant industry in New York. He started as a busboy and was rapidly promoted to waiter, then captain, then manager of one of the finest banquet restaurants in the neighborhood at that time, HSF, on Canal Street. He then left to work at Jumbo Restaurant on Elizabeth Street in 1982, and in 1984 he opened his own restaurant, Village Restaurant, at 66 Mott. He says, "These restaurants changed my life because they were traditional Chinese cuisine, very expensive. Shark's fin soup, abalone, bird's nest, Cantonese classic dishes. They were the best at that time."

He had chosen the restaurants he worked at carefully, for upon arrival he'd noted that at the typical Chinese restaurant in New York, "The cups were heavy and thick, dishes were huge. Big beef balls, huge pork buns. American-style. The quality was poor, and it was not done to top standard." But, says Spencer, this began to change as the immigrants flowed in from China in the seventies and eighties. Originally in New York there were "a lot of people in the restaurant business that were not real chefs. That changed very fast." They wanted to do "something real, real Chinese food. So the whole community upgraded. Plates were more elegant. Those other plates didn't break when you threw them on the floor! Every year it improved."

Spencer soon became the king of innovation in the Chinatown restaurant scene. Opening 20 Mott in 1985, he introduced the first combination seafood and dim sum establishment. He then opened the more upscale Golden Unicorn in 1988, which received rave reviews in the New York press, as had 20 Mott. He says he was the first one to introduce sophisticated presentations and garnishes to the neighborhood. In 1995 Spencer sold Golden Unicorn and focused on creating another new format for 20 Mott. His winning seafood and dim sum combination had been copied several times over at that point, and he was unhappy with the uniformity of the competition and worried that quality would begin to suffer overall in the neighborhood. First he opened a small Sweet-n-Tart Café that sold special dessert soups that had traditional medicinal qualities, among other delights, and introduced the bubble tea phenomena from Taiwan, which was quickly picked up by others in the neighborhood, as is still evident today.

Spencer Chan surveys the kitchen at his Sweet-n-Tart Café in Flushing, Queens.

In 1997 Chan opened a larger Sweet-n-Tart in Flushing, where he tests new recipes—Spencer likes to travel, gathers ideas wherever he goes, then stands beside his chefs in the kitchen to perfect the recipes. His penchant for perfection in the kitchen began when as a captain at Jumbo he would watch the chefs prepare dishes, process and procedure, observing the best way to do things. "Most restaurant owners don't know how, but I can train my chefs. Some chefs are very creative so they can upgrade themselves, but most do not have this creative thinking. I have to push them to upgrade themselves. If a chef says I am a Cantonese chef–doesn't matter. If you can cook, that's fine. You're cooking my style."

By 1999 Spencer was ready to transform 20 Mott into Sweet-n-Tart Restaurant, which remained popular up until 2006 when it was forced to close due to an extremely high increase in rent. But Spencer has not given up on Manhattan's Chinatown, and plans to open a new restaurant there in late 2007. What's next? True to his ability to lead trends, he plans on focusing on Asian fusion, upgrading the style, presentation, and quality even further, and targeting a new, sophisticated set: second- and third-generation Chinese Americans.

BOTTOM: Menus are handwritten on the walls and tea and coffee are served in paper cups at Mei Lai Wah. Beyond the older bachelor clientele, kids arrive after Chinese school, as do many people from the Filipino community, seeking out the roast pork buns. Another treat is their fried dough drizzled with honey. OPPOSITE CENTER: A case filled with fresh almond cookies at Nom Wah. OPPOSITE BOTTOM: Chatham Restaurant, 9 Chatham Square. The rich (and huge) roast pork buns, steamed or baked sit behind the register.

OLD-STYLE COFFEE & TEA HOUSES

老式咖啡館及茶坊

MEI LAI WAH, *64 Bayard Street*

THE ORIGINAL CHINATOWN "COFFEEHOUSES" SERVED AS gathering places and convenient spots for laundry or restaurant workers to stop by for a quick bite of dim sum. Bachelors and senior members of the community could hang out, read the newspaper, and discuss their day. Stepping into Mei Lai Wah or Chatham Restaurant, you think time must have stood still. Ever-present are the stools and booths, the steam and warming cabinets behind the counter filled with steamed or baked roast pork buns, and prices that have also been frozen in time— Mei Lai Wah's topping out at under $2. Order one of their Special Big Buns and you'll receive an extraordinarily filling bun of chicken, pork, egg, and sausage.

NOM WAH TEA PARLOR
13 Doyers Street

NOM WAH, PRESERVED IN A CHOP SUEY—style vein, claims to be the first dim sum parlor in Chinatown, opening in 1920. This establishment is owned by Mr. Wong, who is the third generation to run it. Stop by in the afternoon and you'll find a few customers, perhaps reading the paper or chatting. The atmosphere is calm, perhaps even stagnant, with generations of tea drinking, card playing, cigarette smoking, and dim sum snacking hanging in the air and clinging to the walls––but there's nothing else like it. Their specialty is the large, round almond cookie, taken with a pot of oolong tea. ○

(For more teahouses, see Where to Sip Tea in Chinatown, page 157.)

餐廳 | RESTAURANTS BY CUISINE

中國城的餐館

RESTAURANTS IN CHINATOWN, from tiny dumpling houses to seafood meccas, stretch to the outer limits of the neighborhood, from the central Mott, Pell, and Bayard area, north to Grand Street and southeast to the river—and, for that matter, well beyond into all of the outer New York boroughs' Chinatowns. Several Chinatown restaurants have opened outposts at the end of the Number 7 subway line in Flushing, Queens, for example, where the population tends to be more Taiwanese, the neighborhood can support more upscale dining, and regional cuisines have become the focus. However, solely within Manhattan's historical Chinatown, and the scope of this book, there are more than 500 restaurants to explore. Father Nobiletti jokes, "The occupational hazard down here is the food. The problem is, I like to eat."

This section is by no means comprehensive and is meant to inspire further exploration. As one Chinatown native put it, restaurants in Chinatown are meant for eating. In general the décor is minimal, the atmosphere noisy, the waitstaff sometimes surly, and the lighting less than romantic. But whether the goal is a quick hot bowl of noodles or full-scale family banquet, the focus is on the plate. ○

FORLINI'S, 93 BAXTER STREET

With evidence of the ever-shrinking Little Italy continuing to this day, the northern Italian restaurant Forlini's on Baxter is the last holdout below Canal Street. With a prime location near the courthouses, it's a popular spot for judges, court reporters, and lawyers. Derek, Joe, and Big Joe Forlini run the place their grandfather opened in 1943, and it has been in this location since 1956.

港
式
海
鮮
樓

HONG KONG–STYLE SEAFOOD

FULEEN SEAFOOD, *11 Division Street*

SLIGHTLY OFF THE BEATEN TRACK OF the main tourist center of Chinatown, Fuleen is a local favorite for fresh seafood cooked Hong Kong style, with less oil and more delicate flavors. As one of the owners, Michael Lau, says, "the Chinese like their fish," and true to the Hong Kong tradition they keep it fresh here with live fish tanks and daily shipments.

A Chinatown native and community advocate, Michael is part owner and director of marketing and public relations for Fuleen. In his most recent role, working for the former assistant district attorney for Manhattan's racketeering bureau, the late Gerald Labush, Michael acted as a liaison between the Chinese community and the legal world, tirelessly helping people navigate the system. Walking down the street with Michael, greeting residents and relatives of people he's helped out, you see how Chinatown still retains a small-town feeling.

Dishes to try include: jumbo head-on shrimp stir-fried with sugar snap peas, ginger, red pepper, and garlic; whole bass deep fried and dressed with ginger, scallion, soy sauce, and cilantro; lightly sautéed conch in shrimp sauce over flowering Chinese chives; gently spiced scallops with dried red chili peppers; and a very traditional dish of lotus root, Chinese celery, bean sprouts, pork belly, and carrot. Desserts include sweet, soup-like tapioca with sweet potato and taro and sweet potato slices baked with butter and sugar.

(See the Celebration section, page 125, for banquet recipes courtesy of Fuleen.)

PING SEAFOOD RESTAURANT
22 Mott Street

PING OPENED AS A HONG KONG–STYLE establishment, so aesthetic presentation and freshness is emphasized and more attention is given to the dining room, where cherrywood paneling adorns the walls. The owner, Chung Ping Hui, is a talented chef who hails from Hong Kong as does the manager, Darren Kwong, who takes great pride in "making sure everybody is comfortable, feel good, have great service." Their clientele includes lawyers, doctors, former Mayor Ed Koch, Mayor Mike Bloomberg, and Domenico Dolce and Stefano Gabbana, says Kwong.

Dim sum is popular in this bi-level space, with carts touring the dining room, but their banquet style and seafood dishes are renowned. At Ping you can find winter melon soup, bird's nest soup, shredded squid, and abalone, as well as unusual dishes like duck breast braised in red wine sauce—"only at Ping," Darren says, smiling. "The owner went to a French restaurant" and liked what he had. The menu includes clear photos of the food, which Darren is proud to point out actually comes out looking like the photograph. The fish you eat comes straight from the tanks in the front, adds Darren, "We have everything, good fish tanks. Lobster or crab or fish for customers to look at first, Hong Kong style."

Customers also love Special Ping Fried Rice made with baby shrimp, XO sauce, dried salted fish, green onion, and egg. And for a banquet indulgence, order their shark's fin soup (if budget allows, though there are two price options). It comes individually heated in a covered bowl, a delicacy appropriately enshrined into which you may swirl a dose of the red wine vinegar provided. It has a glutinous, silky texture with delicate flavors of crab meat, chicken broth, and egg.

1. The façade of Fuleen Seafood Restaurant. 2. Michael Lau with his godfather, Mr. Tung Yuen, who is Fuleen's bookkeeper. 3. Fuleen's main dining room. 4. Ping Seafood manager, Darren Kwong. 5 and 6. Ping's façade on Mott Street.

ORIENTAL GARDEN, *14 Elizabeth Street*

FREQUENTED BY UPTOWN NON-CHINESE, chefs, and power-lunching locals, this straightforward restaurant is known for quality seafood and Cantonese specialties. Try the barbecued eel, the razor clams in black bean sauce, steamed whole fish and a variety of noodle dishes with seafood.

Avoid the lines out the door on Sundays, and come for dim sum during the week. Highlights here include smooth taro and pork siu mai

(dumplings presented to look like chicks with sliced almond wings and beaks); large, light and airy fish balls; very rich triangular roast pork pastries with sesame seeds on top; vegetarian rolled-rice noodles exploding with fresh cilantro; stuffed hot peppers with sweet oyster sauce; and steamed milk custard buns with deep creamy yellow centers.

(For more Hong Kong-style dining options, see the Dim Sum and Celebration sections, pages 86 and 125.)

懷舊式餐廳

CHINATOWN CLASSICS

FOR THEIR OWN UNIQUE REASONS, these restaurants fall into a nostalgic category of their own.

DANNY NG, *34 Pell Street*

PHOTOS OF PROPRIETOR DANNY NG with famous people line the walls of this Pell Street standby. The mostly Cantonese offerings (with a twist) boast some surprising dishes like beef in pumpkin, fried chicken with vegetables, baked cheese spring rolls, Thai chicken, and roast beef, as well as a selection of elegant fish and seafood dishes. Try ordering by sight, as the English and Chinese menus are not identical.

HOP KEE RESTAURANT, *21 Mott Street*

A SUBTERRANEAN SPACE ON THE CORNER OF Mosco Street, the bare-bones Hop Kee doesn't look like much, but regulars swear by the specialty dishes (tip: order from the today's specials menu) and appreciate the efficient service. This seventy-year-old institution serves up old-school Toisanese specialties like snails in black bean sauce, Cantonese crab, and steamed minced pork patties in family-style portions. And, for a real nostalgic kick, there are four chop suey dishes on the menu.

WO HOP RESTAURANT, *15 and 17 Mott Street*

WO HOP IS A DESTINATION IN CHINATOWN for those seeking the nostalgic flavors of American-Chinese dishes, in all their greasy, fried glory—and those who have been regulars since it opened in 1976 still stand in line to get in. Yes, "sweet and pungent" pork and a bevy of chow mein, lo mein, and egg foo youngs stand proud on the menu. In this day and age of regional, refined cuisine preferences, Wo Hop is a comfort to those who secretly bemoan the loss of huge, cheap platters and portions in Chinatown. Upstairs has more of a typical Chinatown atmosphere, while downstairs is more cramped and noisy.

BELOW: Mr. Chan and a few of his staff members.
RIGHT: Mr. Chan's Roast Pork is marinated with hoisin, bean sauce, sugar, salt, and ginger for two hours, after which it is skewered and roasted.

港
式
燒
烤

CANTONESE BARBECUE

HSIN WONG, *72 Bayard Street*

CANTONESE BARBECUE IS A STAPLE LUNCH in Chinatown, witness the hanging ducks, pork, and chicken in so many of the restaurant windows. Regulars come by to pick up their meats as a quick and easy meal for their families or stop by for sliced meats over rice. Hsin Wong is one such favored spot. Mr. Chan, proprietor and twenty-year veteran of Chinatown restaurants, has staff members come in at five in the morning to start preparing the meat, none of which has ever been frozen. Below, he takes us through the steps in making the delectable morsels.

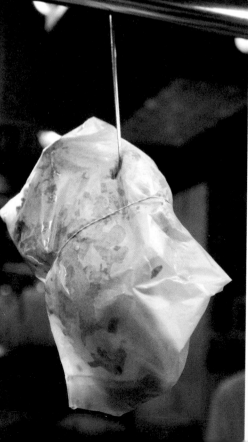

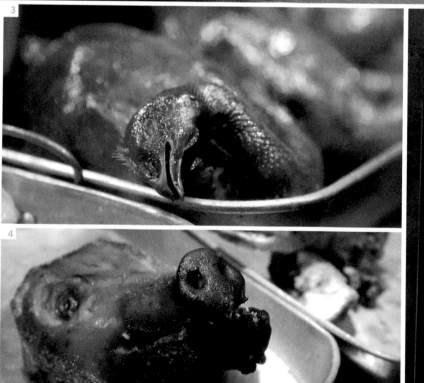

GREAT N.Y. NOODLETOWN, *28½ Bowery*

ANOTHER BARBECUE SPOT, late-night favorite Great N.Y. Noodletown excels in roast meats over noodles in soup, as well as a wide range of rice and pan-fried and lo mein noodles. Other highlights are Chinese flowering chive with duck and salt-baked shrimp, squid, and scallops.

1. At Hsin Wong, Mr. Chan makes his roast duck by stuffing it with a seasoning mixture of pepper, ginger powder, salt, and sugar, tying up the opening with kitchen twine and then soaking the duck in boiling water flavored with vinegar, salt, malt sugar, and sesame oil. It is then air-dried for two hours, which promotes cripy skin, and roasted for forty-five minutes. 2. This succulent Boiled Chicken with Ginger and Scallion Sauce is made by simmering the chicken in an herbal stock until cooked, after which it is roasted for 15 minutes, then covered in a ginger and scallion mixture and placed in a wax-paper bag to rest for one hour. 3. Roasted soy sauce chicken. 4. Pig and duck heads for sale in the window. 5. Take-out at Great N.Y. Noodletown.

飲茶 DIM SUM

FOR MANY NEW YORKERS, dim sum is the reason for a trip to Chinatown. No visit is complete without a cart of steaming dumplings rolling by communal tables, the din of family chatter, and cup after cup of tea.

Sundays are hands-down the most popular day for dim sum, for both Chinese families and others—and that can mean lines at some of the more well-known establishments. But as anyone who's had jury duty and scooted over to Chinatown during the break for lunch knows, dim sum is not served only as a sort of weekend brunch, but as breakfast and lunch during the week as well. On any given midweek morning you'll find older Chinatown residents reading their newspapers and chatting for hours over dim sum and tea, perhaps after their morning exercises in the park. It is said that the tradition began in teahouses built to nourish weary travelers along the Silk Road. Local farmers would also drop by after work for tea, and eventually they added small bites to eat to their offerings. The term *yum cha*, or to drink tea, is thus used interchangeably to mean the eating of dim sum. There is evidence in artwork of dim sum being consumed as early as the tenth century, the beginning of the Sung dynasty.

What constitutes dim sum varies by restaurant and by regional focus. It is generally considered a Cantonese specialty, but non-Cantonese restaurants have embraced the trend, adding their own twists to the selections, and what is now considered traditional dim sum consists of dishes from all over China. Classic items are shrimp dumplings (*har gau*), pork and shrimp dumplings (*siu mai*), steamed pork buns (*char siu bau*), chicken feet, lotus leaf rice (*nor mai gao*), turnip cake with oyster sauce, and sweets like small egg custard tarts or mango pudding.

Dim sum tends to be an extremely thrifty choice. Each dish is marked down on a card for your table as you pick it from the cart, and

A FEW TIPS FOR DIM SUM DINING

• If the restaurant is of the cart-serving variety, reverse what your mother taught you about table preference—smart regulars seat themselves near the door to the kitchen to catch the freshest dishes and ensure they don't miss out on any delicacies.

• Go in large groups. Dim sum (which means "touch the heart") is meant to be shared, and you get to try more of the offerings.

• Always pour tea for others at the table before yourself. If someone serves you, it is customary to tap two fingers next to your cup to show thanks. This custom comes from the legend of an emperor who went out of the palace to inspect the countryside disguised as a peasant. His ministers could not reveal his identity, so when he poured them tea at the teahouse they "kowtowed" to him with their fingers to show respect.

• If your teapot is empty and you would like more, simply turn the top upside down or askew, and the waiter will give you a fresh pot. Black Pu-erh tea is most common, as it is known to aid digestion of the sometimes rich food.

• If you wish to cut something in half to share, or if you're reaching to take an item off a serving plate, etiquette dictates that you flip your chopsticks around and use the thicker part to perform the task.

TOP: Jing Fong in full dim sum mode. CENTER LEFT: Mandarin Court. CENTER RIGHT: Golden Unicorn. ABOVE: Dishing up dumplings at Ping.

the price per person rarely totals more than $10 for a meal by the end. Not all Chinatown restaurants are this inexpensive, or use the carts, but the largest halls tend to follow both rules. Almost everyone has an opinion about which dim sum is the best among the tremendous number of options——and customers tend to be very loyal.

A FEW STANDOUTS TO EXPLORE IN CHINATOWN

DIM SUM GOGO, 5 *East Broadway*
A sleek space and beautiful assortment of dumplings with unusual fillings. No carts. **(see recipes starting on page 90)**

GOLDEN UNICORN, 18 *East Broadway*
A wide selection of choices (with pictures), two floors of seating, and loads of carts.

JING FONG, 20 *Elizabeth Street*
The largest banquet-style restaurant, a circus of bustling classic dim sum. Carts.

MANDARIN COURT RESTAURANT, 61 *Mott Street*
A perennial favorite. Try the scallop dumplings, lotus seed buns, and chicken turnovers. Carts.

ORIENTAL GARDEN, 14 *Elizabeth Street*
An upscale option with a seafood specialty. Come early to avoid the lines. No carts.

PING, 22 *Mott Street*
Elegant, with unusual choices such as fruit seafood roll and sesame chopped ribs. Carts.

SUNRISE 27, 27 *Division Street*
Traditional cart-style dim sum, popular with the locals.

VEGETARIAN DIM SUM HOUSE, 24 *Pell Street*
Creative dim sum is served all day, all vegetarian with "mock" meat choices. No carts.

VERONICA LEUNG

DIM SUM GOGO, *5 East Broadway*

DIM SUM AFICIONADOS WOULD AGREE THAT one way to test a restaurant is to order their dumplings: How much shrimp or scallops versus vegetable filling is used? How carefully are the dumplings folded, and how refined is the dumpling dough? Dim Sum GoGo's dumplings are some of the most artful in the neighborhood, executed in the new Hong Kong–style with a wide range of ingredients.

At the helm of this slick space, decorated in white with red accents and matte metal chairs, is the energetic and charming manager, Veronica Leung. She has fashioned her dim sum after the sophisticated Hong Kong restaurants that experiment with varieties of ingredients and exquisite selections. The restaurant opened in 2000, originally with Hong Kong chef Guy Liv and food writer Colette Rossant, and Veronica is very proud that it has managed to remain consistent. Unusual for Chinatown, she keeps two full chefs in the kitchen, not just one chef and line cooks, so that the quality remains high if one of them can't be there.

Beyond dim sum, she features what she considers "Cantonese home cooking, no cornstarch-thick sauces and not oily." Fresh vegetables and meats are delivered every day, and it comes out in the cooking. The chives, crab, and pea shoots pop with flavor. "I miss Mommy's home cooking," Veronica says, and regrets not having stood by her side to learn, but she did learn how to eat and those taste memories have never left her. So, working side by side with the chef to develop some of the recipes, she has brought back some of the maternal flavors. One such dish is the Abbot's Delight, a Shanghainese dried turnip and pickled mustard green dish that her mother used to serve over congee—only here they put it inside a dumpling. Other standouts include a delectable, comforting chicken casserole with taro and Chinese sausage, sautéed

ABOVE: Veronica Leung at Dim Sum GoGo. **OPPOSITE BOTTOM LEFT:** Veronica provides a little dish of roasted nuts for munching and condiments crafted to add another dimension of flavor to the already well-seasoned dumplings.

tender sliced beef with house-made preserved young ginger, and GoGo Seafood with lotus root and white fungus with Chinese broccoli (ladies, the fungus is good for your complexion, says Veronica).

Veronica's culinary connection goes beyond her mother's apron strings, however. In the 1950s her father was one of seven Hong Kong chefs to be brought to New York to work at an upscale restaurant called House of Chan, the first Chinese restaurant in Midtown. The rest of her family came a few years later. Her father left his mark at the House of Chan, creating chicken wings, which were normally thrown away, as an appetizer. They are still a staple of pupu platters around the city. Eventually her father bought a restaurant in Schenectady. At first neither she nor any of her siblings wanted to go into the restaurant industry, having seen their parents work fourteen-hour days. But after years in the garment industry, in which she'd entertain European buyers with live shrimp boils in the showrooms that had kitchens, Veronica decided to embrace the family business with Dim Sum GoGo. She feels she did the right thing. She says she's worked "six years without a day off, but you still see a happy face. What is most important is people's appreciation of the food."

Traditionally, regular soy sauce is never placed directly on the table when serving dumplings. As Veronica says, "Soy sauce kills it; all you taste is soy sauce." Each dumpling or dim sum has a particular sauce that complements it and will be served appropriately, for example oyster sauce on slices of turnip cake, or sweet soy, vinegar, and scallion sauce for potstickers.

Veronica serves her dumplings with a bright blend of fresh ginger and scallions; a tangy, salty mixture of dried shrimp and scallops with chili pepper; and vinegar and garlic.

SIU MAI

Veronica notes that to lighten the dumplings, the chef uses lean pork instead of the traditional fattier cuts, and shrimp are added to replace the moisture from the fat.

Makes about 30 dumplings

Ingredients:

9 ounces ground lean pork

5 ounces shelled and deveined shrimp, diced fine

½ teaspoon salt

½ teaspoon chicken bouillon granules

1½ teaspoons cornstarch

1 teaspoon peanut or vegetable oil

1 teaspoon sugar

1 ounce dried black shiitake mushrooms, soaked, drained, and minced (about ⅔ cup when done)

2 teaspoons sesame oil, or to taste

⅓ package store-bought dumpling wrappers

Blanched cabbage, lettuce, or bok choy leaves for steaming (optional)

Golden tobiko for garnish (optional)

Directions:

1. In a bowl combine the pork, shrimp, salt, bouillon granules, cornstarch, oil and stir with a wooden spoon until blended well. Add the sugar and 2 teaspoons water and blend again. Add the mushrooms and sesame oil and stir to combine.

2. To make each dumpling, place 2 teaspoons of the filling into the center of a dumpling wrapper. Gather the edges of the dough up around the filling and with a small round spoon, pack down the filling, smoothing the top. Squeeze the dough lightly to create a "neck" to keep dumpling and filling intact during cooking.

3. Arrange the dumplings ½ inch apart on an oiled bamboo or metal steaming rack. (The stackable bamboo version can be found at restaurant supply stores; also see Online and Phone Resources on page 216.) The rack may be lined with blanched leaves to prevent the dumplings from sticking. Place the steamer rack in a wok or large wide saucepan on top of the stove. Fill the pan with enough water so that the bottom of the steamer, where the dumplings rest, sits evenly above but not touching water. If using a saucepan, it may be necessary to invert a ramekin or small dish under the steamer. Over high heat, bring the water to a boil, cover the pan, and steam 10 minutes. Garnish with caviar, if desired.

CHIVE DUMPLINGS

Note that while most dumplings freeze well, these dumplings do not due to the chives.

Makes about 30 dumplings

Ingredients:

6 ounces shelled and deveined shrimp, minced

½ teaspoon salt

½ teaspoon chicken bouillon granules

2 teaspoons cornstarch

1 teaspoon sugar

8 ounces Chinese garlic chives, cut into ½-inch lengths
   Freshly ground black pepper to taste

2 teaspoons peanut or vegetable oil

1 to 2 teaspoons sesame oil, or to taste

1 recipe Wheat Starch Dough (page 92) rolled into 3-inch
   round wrappers or ⅓ package store-bought dumpling
   wrappers

Blanched cabbage, lettuce, or bok choy leaves for steaming
   (optional)

Directions:

1. In a bowl combine the shrimp, salt, bouillon granules, and 1 teaspoon of the cornstarch and stir until blended. Cover the bowl with plastic and chill for 1 hour.

2. Drain the mixture, if necessary, and transfer it to a clean bowl. Add the sugar, chives, pepper, peanut oil, sesame oil, and remaining cornstarch and stir to combine well.

3. To make each dumpling, place 1½ teaspoons of the filling into the center of a round of dough. Gather the edges of the dough together to cover the filling and twist to seal at the top, making a round bundle.

4. Arrange the dumplings ½ inch apart on an oiled bamboo or metal steaming rack. (The stackable bamboo version can be found at restaurant supply stores; Also see Online and Phone Resources on page 216.) (The racks may be lined with blanched leaves to prevent the dumplings from sticking.) Place the steamer rack in a wok or large wide saucepan on top of the stove. Fill the pan with enough water so that the bottom of the steamer, where the dumplings rest, sits evenly above but not touching water. If using a saucepan, it may be necessary to invert a ramekin or small dish under the steamer. Over high heat, bring the water to a boil, cover the pan, and steam 7 minutes.

WHEAT STARCH DOUGH

As this dough dries out quickly, be sure to keep any unused dough wrapped in plastic. If you have a tortilla press, you're in luck—it will produce the perfect thickness. Just grease the balls a little bit before pressing. Note that this dumpling dough, in comparison with the premade wrappers, is much more delicate, soft, and glutinous.

Makes enough dough for 28 to 30 three-inch round dumplings.

Ingredients:

1 cup wheat starch, plus extra for dusting

½ cup tapioca starch

½ cup cornstarch

¼ teaspoon salt

1¼ cups boiling water

1 tablespoon peanut oil

All-purpose flour for kneading

Directions:

1. In a bowl combine the wheat starch, tapioca starch, cornstarch and salt. With chopsticks or a wooden spoon, stir in the boiling water and the oil until the mixture forms a dough in the bowl. While still warm turn the dough out onto a lightly floured board and knead it until smooth. Cut the dough in half and wrap each half in plastic. Let sit 30 minutes.

2. Working with one ball of dough at a time (keep the other ball half wrapped in plastic), roll it into a log about 14 inches long. Cut the log into 1-inch pieces. Roll each piece into a ball and with the palm of your hand flatten each into a round. Transfer the rounds to a plate lightly dusted with wheat starch and cover with plastic wrap.

3. Lightly dust the work surface and a rolling pin with wheat starch. Working with one round of dough at a time, roll the dough into a 3-inch circle, or use a tortilla press. The edges should be thinner than the center. Transfer the wrappers to a plate and cover with plastic until ready to be filled.

PRESERVED VEGETABLE DUMPLINGS

Makes about 30 dumplings

Ingredients:

4 ounces preserved mustard greens

½ cup minced button mushrooms

2 or 3 spears asparagus, minced (¼ cup)

½ ounce tree ear fungus, soaked, drained, and minced
　(⅓ cup; see note)

⅓ cup canned minced bamboo shoots

⅓ cup minced carrot

⅓ cup minced celery

2 tablespoons peanut oil

2 teaspoons minced fresh ginger

1 clove garlic, minced

½ teaspoon salt, or to taste

2 to 3 teaspoons sugar, to taste

Freshly ground black pepper to taste

2 teaspoons sesame oil, or to taste

1 tablespoon Shao Hsing wine
　(or any rice wine, sake, or dry Sherry), or to taste

1 tablespoon cornstarch dissolved in 2 tablespoons
　cold water

1 recipe Wheat Starch Dough (see page 92) rolled into
　3-inch round wrappers or ⅓ package store-bought
　dumpling wrappers

Blanched cabbage, lettuce, or bok choy leaves for steaming
　(optional)

Directions:

1. Cut the mustard greens horizontally into thin strips and soak in a bowl of water for 15 minutes. Meanwhile, bring a pot of water to a boil.

2. Drain the mustard greens. Combine the greens, mushrooms, asparagus, tree ear fungus, bamboo shoots, carrot, and celery in a strainer and blanch in boiling water for 1 minute. Drain and run under cold water. Drain again. Spread out on paper towels to air dry.

3. In a wok set over medium-high heat, heat the peanut oil until hot but not smoking. Add the ginger and garlic and stir-fry 30 seconds. Add the vegetables, salt, sugar, black pepper, sesame oil, and wine and stir-fry 1 minute. Stir the cornstarch mixture and add it to the wok a little at a time, until the mixture is thickened. Let cool.

4. Place 1½ teaspoons of the filling into the center of each round of dough. Gather the edges of the dough together to cover the filling and twist to seal at the top, making a round bundle.

5. Arrange the dumplings ½ inch apart on an oiled bamboo or metal steaming rack. (The stackable bamboo version can be found at restaurant supply stores; see Resources on page 211.) The racks may be lined with blanched leaves to prevent the dumplings from sticking. Place the steamer in a wok or large wide saucepan on top of the stove. Fill the pan with enough water so that the bottom of the steamer, where the dumplings rest, sits evenly above but not touching water. If using a saucepan, it may be necessary to invert a ramekin or small dish under the steamer. Over high heat, bring the water to a boil, cover the pan, and steam 8 minutes.

Note: **Substitute cloud ears or shiitakes if tree ear fungus is not available.**

Preserved mustard greens.

SHREDDED DUCK DUMPLINGS

If you like, you can purchase cooked duck breast from a Chinese restaurant for this recipe. Make sure that you include the crispy skin in the filling for flavor and moisture.

Makes about 30 dumplings

Ingredients:

½ cup minced button mushrooms

4 to 6 asparagus spears, minced (½ cup)

⅓ cup minced celery

½ ounce tree ear fungus, soaked, drained, and minced
   (⅓ cup; see note)

⅓ cup canned minced bamboo shoots

⅓ cup minced carrot

1 tablespoon peanut or vegetable oil

2 teaspoons minced fresh ginger

½ teaspoon salt, or to taste

¼ teaspoon chicken bouillon granules

¼ teaspoon sugar

1 teaspoon soy sauce

Freshly ground black pepper to taste

2 teaspoons sesame oil, or to taste

1 tablespoon Shao Hsing wine (or any rice wine, sake, or
   dry Sherry), or to taste

1 tablespoon cornstarch dissolved in 2 tablespoons
   cold water

5 ounces shredded cooked duck meat
   (about ½ duck breast with skin)

⅓ package store-bought dumpling wrappers

Blanched cabbage, lettuce, or bok choy leaves for steaming
   (optional)

Directions:

1. Bring a large pot of water to a boil.

2. Combine the mushrooms, asparagus, celery, tree ear fungus, bamboo shoots, and carrot in a strainer and blanch for 1 minute. Drain and run under cold water. Drain again. Spread the ingredients out on paper towels to air dry.

3. In a wok set over medium-high heat, heat the peanut oil until hot but not smoking. Add the ginger and stir-fry 30 seconds. Add the vegetables, salt, bouillon granules, sugar, soy sauce, black pepper, sesame oil and wine and stir-fry 1 minute. Stir the cornstarch mixture and add it to the wok a little at a time until the mixture is thickened. Let cool. Add the duck and stir well to combine.

4. To make each dumpling, place 1½ teaspoons of the filling into the center of a round of dough and fold the dough in half to form a half-moon shape. Hold the dumpling in your left hand and begin to form pleats with the fingers of your right hand along the curve of the crescent. Continue to form small pleats until the dumpling is completely closed. Press the top pleated edge of the dumpling to seal it tightly.

5. Arrange the dumplings ½ inch apart on an oiled bamboo or metal steaming rack. (The stackable bamboo version can be found at restaurant supply stores; see Resources on page 211.) The racks may be lined with blanched leaves to prevent the dumplings from sticking. Place the steamer in a wok or large wide saucepan on top of the stove. Fill the pan with enough water so that the bottom of the steamer, where the dumplings rest, sits evenly above but not touching water. If using a saucepan, it may be necessary to invert a ramekin or small dish under the steamer. Over high heat, bring the water to a boil, cover the pan and steam 7 minutes.

Note: **Substitute cloud ears or shiitakes if tree ear fungus is not available.**

THREE-STAR DUMPLINGS

Makes about 30 dumplings

Ingredients:

1 cup finely diced lotus root, fresh or canned

⅔ cup finely diced jicama

½ cup minced button mushrooms

3 or 4 spears asparagus, minced (⅓ cup)

½ ounce tree ear fungus, soaked, drained, and minced
   (see note)

⅓ cup canned minced bamboo shoots

2 tablespoons peanut or vegetable oil

2 teaspoons minced fresh ginger

½ teaspoon salt

1 teaspoon sugar

Freshly ground black pepper to taste

1 teaspoon soy sauce, or to taste

2 teaspoons sesame oil, or to taste

1 tablespoon Shao Hsing wine
   (or any rice wine, sake, or dry Sherry), or to taste

1 tablespoon cornstarch dissolved in 2 tablespoons
   cold water

1 recipe Wheat Starch Dough (see recipe page 92),
   made with a few drops beet juice (optional) in the
   boiling water for color, rolled into 3-inch round
   wrappers or ⅓ package store-bought dumpling wrappers

Blanched cabbage, lettuce, or bok choy leaves for steaming
   (optional)

Directions:

1. Bring a large pot of water to a boil.

2. Combine the lotus root, jicama, mushrooms, asparagus, tree ear fungus, and bamboo shoots in a strainer and blanch for 1 minute. Drain and run under cold water. Drain again. Spread the ingredients out on paper towels to air dry.

3. In a wok set over medium high heat, heat the peanut oil until hot but not smoking. Add the ginger and stir-fry 30 seconds. Add the vegetables, salt, sugar, black pepper, soy sauce, sesame oil, and wine and stir-fry 1 minute. Stir the cornstarch mixture and add it to the wok a little at a time until mixture is thickened. Let cool.

4. To make each dumpling, place 1½ teaspoons of the filling into the center of a round of dough. Gather the edges of the dough together to cover the filling and twist to seal at the top, making a round bundle.

5. Arrange the dumplings ½ inch apart on an oiled bamboo or metal steaming rack. (The stackable bamboo version can be found at restaurant supply stores; see Resources on page 211.) The racks may be lined with blanched leaves to prevent the dumplings from sticking. Place the steamer in a wok or large wide saucepan on top of the stove. Fill the pan with enough water so that the bottom of the steamer, where the dumplings rest, sits evenly above but not touching water. If using a saucepan, it may be necessary to invert a ramekin or small dish under the steamer. Over high heat, bring the water to a boil, cover the steaming racks and steam 7 minutes.

Note: Substitute cloud ears or shiitakes if tree ear fungus is not available.

MAY MAY GOURMET CHINESE DELICACIES
35 Pell Street

CONTINUING A BUSINESS STARTED BY his father in 1965, John
Hung of May May makes high-quality dim sum that are sold frozen and
ready to steam. He sells them directly out of his retail store on Pell
Street as well as to commercial outlets. May May offerings include mango and crab dim sum, jumbo shrimp and watercress dim sum, steamed
pork buns, lotus seed buns, spring rolls, and Chinese "pita bread" that
are used with Peking duck dishes.

The Hung family history follows a familiar path, but a very successful one. They arrived in the United States in 1962, when John Hung was
ten or eleven, under the sponsorship of his aunt, and went to work for
the aunt at her laundry in Jackson Heights, Queens. The family had run
coffee shops in Hong Kong, and after a year Hung's father saved enough
money to pay back the aunt and landed a job as head baker in a Chinatown coffee shop. John and his two brothers would go to school, then go
directly to the coffee shop to help their father. They saw it as a chance to
continue in the baking profession, an apprenticeship, but "the boss was
also lucky," John points out. "We helped with no pay!" They spent two
years with his father, working fourteen hours a day, seven days a week.
But their attitude was positive, and John remembers thinking, "It's okay,
our product demands it. This is going to be our future." There were no
days off, and if it was a weekend or a holiday it was even more busy. The

OPPOSITE PAGE: May May's façade on the south side of Pell. ABOVE CLOCKWISE: John is featured on an episode of the children's show *Arthur*, and children often greet him when he's spotted at his store. Boiling "Chinese tamales." These little packages are sticky rice with a meat or vegetable filling, wrapped in bamboo leaves and cooked. The door to this area is often open to the street, and the sweet fragrance wafts out onto the sidewalk, enticing passersby.

toughest period was high school, recalls John. "You want to take a girl out to go bowling, and you can't because there's so much work to do!" And his only outlet for sport was to squeeze in a little Ping-Pong here and there.

John's very talented father was able to open his own business in record time and grew his bakery from a small store in 1964 to a 20,000-square-foot factory, the first one in the United States that mass-produced steam buns. Over the years they began to make lotus seed buns, red bean buns, and the "Chinese tamales," as they started to see what people wanted.

In 1975 John quit school and took over the business from his ailing father. He laughs, "It's been forty-one years. Look what I've got—a bald head. There's always a price to pay."

As Chinatown changes, John looks to capture trends and the market demands of the neighborhood, explaining, "In the mid-eighties, for example, vegetarian products began to become popular and I was able to capture that market." He sees his food as reminiscent of "grandma food"—made by the kind of woman who gets up early to "make little morsels for kids to take to school," but also as convenience food that people can easily heat up and serve to guests.

Here he shares the recipe for one of his best sellers, Spinach and Vegetable Dim Sum. And if you're not up for making them, you can always order them at www.MayMayfood.com.

SPINACH AND VEGETABLE DIM SUM

Adapted from a recipe courtesy of John Hung, May May

Makes about 30 dumplings

Ingredients:

½ cup minced cooked Shanghai cabbage or baby bok choy

½ cup minced cooked spinach

½ cup minced cooked broccoli

¼ cup minced cooked watercress

¼ cup minced cooked carrot

½ ounce tree ear fungus, soaked, drained, and minced
(⅓ cup reconstituted; see note)

⅓ cup minced pickled vegetable, such as mustard greens

1 tablespoon sesame oil

1 tablespoon light soy sauce

½ teaspoon sugar

¼ teaspoon ground white pepper

⅓ package fresh spinach dumpling wrappers
(or regular dumpling wrappers)

Blanched cabbage, lettuce, or bok choy leaves for steaming
(optional)

Directions:

1. In a bowl combine all the ingredients except the dumpling wrappers.

To make each dumpling, place 1½ teaspoons of the filling into the center of a wrapper. Gather the edges of the dough up around the filling and with a small round spoon pack down the filling, smoothing the top. Squeeze the dough lightly to create a "neck" to keep the dumpling and filling intact during cooking.

2. Arrange the dumplings ½ inch apart on an oiled bamboo or metal steaming rack. (The stackable bamboo version can be found at restaurant supply stores; see Resources on page 216.) The rack may be lined with blanched leaves to prevent the dumplings from sticking. Place the steamer in a wok or large wide saucepan on top of the stove. Fill the pan with enough water so that the bottom of the steamer, where the dumplings rest, sits evenly above but not touching water. If using a saucepan, it may be necessary to invert a ramekin or small dish under the steamer. Over high heat, bring the water to a boil, cover the pan and steam 10 minutes.

Note: Substitute cloud ears or shiitakes if tree ear fungus is not available.

TOP: Two brands of chicken bouillon powder. ABOVE: Dumpling wrappers for sale at Po Wing Hong.

麵、水餃、粥

Noodles, Dumplings, and Congee

FRIED DUMPLING, *106 Mosco Street*

FIVE PORK DUMPLINGS FOR $1. It's a simple concept, definitely on the greasy side but flavorful, and there's no pretension here. They fly out the door. The buns, four for $1, are less greasy. Also worth a try: their sister restaurant at 99 Allen Street, Tasty Dumpling at 54 Mulberry Street, and Dumpling House at 118A Eldridge Street.

NEW WONTON GARDEN, *56 Mott Street*

POPULAR WITH BROADWAY ACTORS for years (it's open until 2 AM), this restaurant offers boiled egg noodles and wontons in copious amounts bathed in flavorful chicken broth. Other highlights are pork and shrimp dumplings and curry beef stew over noodles. The Lau family opened for business in 1980 and oversees everything, down to the mixing of the chili sauce condiments at the table.

YUMMY NOODLE, *48 Bowery*

A BUSTLING, sure-footed standby for its variety of clay-pot rice casseroles, wonton, chow fun, and roast meats. Also offers congee and more at the requisite cheap prices.

CONGEE, *98 Bowery*

WHILE PLACES LIKE HSIN WONG and New York Noodletown also offer congee, this spot dedicates itself to it. The comfort-food dish is essentially a rice porridge, often served for breakfast, that takes on the flavorings of whatever you like to add, for example, salty preserved egg, mixed seafood, or roast pork.

Also worth a try: New Wing Wong at 111 Lafayette Street.
For more stylish, kitschy surroundings, and a hip little cocktail/juice bar, try Congee Village at 100 Allen Street.

上海 SHANGHAINESE

SHANGHAI CAFÉ, *100 Mott Street*

OF THE SHANGHAI RESTAURANTS in the neighborhood, Shanghai Café wins the hearts of the young. With a funky neon-lit décor, cheap prices, and great food, it attracts crowds seeking the tender and juicy soup dumplings, shredded turnip cakes, braised sea cucumber, long-cooked and rich roast pork, and chewy, thick Shanghai lo mein noodles (based on egg, not flour).

SHANGHAI SOUP DUMPLINGS

Shanghai Café's legendary steamed tiny buns or soup dumplings (xiao long bao) are assembled and steamed in the front of the restaurant, seemingly without pause—in fact, more than 1,600 dumplings a day are made and sold. How they manage to get soup in the center of the dumplings is a closely guarded secret (I'm guessing a gelatinous reduced stock or aspic in the filling), but here is the process by which they're made:

1. Balls of dumpling dough are flattened gently and rolled thin with a dowel until they're flattened into round wrappers. 2. Pork and shrimp filling is placed in the center of the dough. 3. The dumpling dough is folded and twisted into a small pouch. 4. The dumplings are placed on a bed of Napa cabbage leaves, to prevent sticking, in a bamboo steamer. 5. The dumplings are served immediately with a sweet soy, vinegar, and scallion dipping sauce. 6. To eat a soup dumpling, you must first place the spoon underneath the dumpling and bite off a bit of the top. Gently suck some of the broth out of the dumpling, and any extra juices are caught by the spoon. Be careful, as the broth inside can be quite hot.

PORK SHOULDER IN BROWN SAUCE

Adapted from a recipe courtesy of Shanghai Café

Grace Lau, an owner of Shanghai Café, shares this rich, classic, incredibly tender Shanghai-style roast pork dish. Note that you need a very large pot to fry the pork shoulder, as it displaces a lot of oil.

Makes 6 servings

Ingredients:

1 quart peanut oil for deep frying

3½ to 4 pounds bone-in, unskinned, pork shoulder, rinsed and patted dry

2 cups light soy sauce

1 cup Shao Hsing wine, sake, or dry Sherry

¼ pound Chinese rock sugar
   (or granulated sugar if not available)

2 ounces peeled and sliced fresh ginger

2 tablespoons cornstarch dissolved in ¼ cup cold water
   (if needed)

1 pound Shanghai cabbage or baby bok choy, steamed, as an accompaniment

Directions:

1. In a large casserole or Dutch oven, set over medium-high heat, heat the oil to 320°F. Add the pork shoulder and fry on all sides for 10 minutes in all, or until the skin is golden. Carefully transfer the pork to a bowl filled with ice water and let cool. Drain.

2. In a large casserole over high heat, bring 10 cups of water, the soy sauce, rice wine, sugar, and ginger to a boil. Add the pork and cook at a vigorous simmer, uncovered, for 1¼ to 1½ hours, until pork is tender.

3. If the sauce is not thickened and almost completely reduced at this point, transfer the pork to a plate and reduce the cooking liquid to 2 cups. Add the cornstarch and water mixture to the simmering cooking liquid and simmer until lightly thickened. Return pork to casserole and simmer until heated through. Serve with Shanghai cabbage.

MORE SHANGHAINESE SPOTS

GOODIES, *1 East Broadway*

Beyond soup dumplings, other specialties include whole prawns in pepper sauce, scallion pancakes and five-flavor beef.

JOE'S SHANGHAI, *9 Pell Street*

Well known for leading the neighborhood into the soup dumpling craze, along with a brother restaurant, Joe's Ginger (113 Mott). Try their braised sea cucumber and dongbo pork.

NEW GREEN BO, *66 Bayard Street*

While yet again the dumplings are perhaps the most popular thing on the menu, try the fried yellow fish and twice-cooked pork.

 # VEGETARIAN

素
食

CHINESE VEGETARIAN FOOD has roots going back to 400 AD, when a Buddhist emperor, Liang Wu, entered a monastery late in life. He encouraged the development of all-vegetarian dishes served at the monastery into an art form—and art it is. Through the use of a wide variety of ingredients, such as seitan, mushroom stems, tofu skin, taro, and wheat gluten and an intricate array of spices, Chinese vegetarian recipes actually mimic the flavor and texture of meat and fish.

VEGETARIAN DIM SUM HOUSE
24 Pell Street

FRANKIE, THE PROPRIETOR OF Vegetarian Dim Sum House, came to the United States in 1982. His father, a carpenter who built tables and chairs for export, had moved the family to Hong Kong from Canton for four or five years before bringing them to New York. Frankie entered high school in Bay Ridge, and found a job after school as a busboy in a restaurant on Mott, an experience that helped him "learn how to open a restaurant and how to make it." But it was his brother's experience in a vegetarian restaurant in Hong Kong that inspired Frankie, his three brothers and four sisters to open House of Vegetarian at 64 Mott Street in 1986. It was the first vegetarian restaurant in Chinatown.

The restaurant was a success, and the family went on to open Vegetarian Dim Sum House ten years later. Opening a dim sum restaurant is a different kind of challenge. Dim sum is labor-intensive and specialized, with cooks arriving at 3 AM to prep for the day. Making vegetarian dim sum is doubly difficult, with all of the techniques and processes to follow to mimic meats. Frankie knows this all too well. One day he

TOP: Frankie outside the restaurant on Pell Street.
CENTER: Roast "pork" over Chinese broccoli. BOTTOM: Fried "shrimp."

abruptly lost his dim sum chef and had to learn how to make the dim sum himself over the course of seventeen hours. "People were laughing at me," Frankie chuckles. But he persevered for three months until he found a replacement—and he's even come up with some (closely guarded) recipes himself.

Vegetarian Dim Sum House is remarkably delicious and recommended for wary meat eaters who will, no doubt, be impressed with the flavors and textures.

TOP: Buddha Bodai on Mott street. **RIGHT:** In the basement kitchen of Golden Seafood, cooking at very high temperatures over a traditionally designed Chinese stove—which today essentially consists of deep-set and very hot jet gas ranges over which the rounded wok is placed. **BOTTOM RIGHT:** Plating in the kitchen at Golden Seafood.

MORE VEGETARIAN OPTIONS

BUDDHA BODAI, 5 Mott Street
Traditional Chinese vegetarian dishes such as roast pork, jellyfish in sesame oil, pineapple chicken, and crispy eel with broccoli served in a very aesthetically pleasing manner. This is the only certified kosher restaurant in Chinatown.

18 ARHANS RESTAURANT, 227 Centre Street
A Buddhist temple that also serves take-out vegetarian selections; it has a small seating area.

FOR MORE SPECIALTIES and ingredients for Chinese vegetarian cuisine, including some astonishing soy-based "faux meat" products, visit May Wah Healthy Vegetarian Food, 213 Hester Street.

FUJIAN 福建

OF COURSE WITH THE HUGE INFLUX of immigrants from Fujian province in recent years, restaurants representing this little-known cuisine have followed. Stroll down East Broadway, and you'll no doubt pick up on the fact that the Fujianese are known for their seafood. Other notable Fujian foods include noodles served in broth with meat and fish balls. A lot of Fujian food is cooked in stock, rather than stir-fried, and herbs are seldom used. Fu Chow sauce, a sweet-and-sour sauce made from red rice wine paste (left over from making wine) is commonly used. Most Fujian families make the wine themselves, so finding the sauce for sale can be a challenge, but it can be located in rows of unmarked plastic containers outside shops and some restaurants along East Broadway.

GOLDEN SEAFOOD RESTAURANT
40 East Broadway

GOLDEN SEAFOOD IS AN UPSCALE Fujian seafood restaurant on East Broadway. While the menu features Cantonese items as well, steer toward the seafood selections, the more unfamiliar the better. Conch is a specialty, as is sweet-and-sour chrysanthemum fish (a banquet favorite), fried fish with "special sauce," and the marvelously smooth, tender, and sweet egg with pearl clam soup.

TOP: Manager Qiyong Chen surveys the scene with an attentive eye. Mr. Chen is both the manager of Golden Seafood and Chairman of the American Fujian Association of Commerce and Industry. 1. Conch with asparagus and fried tofu. 2. Fish maw with sugar snap peas, asparagus, and mushroom. 3. Conch in Fu Chow sauce.

NAM ZHOU HAND MADE NOODLE AND DUMPLING PLACE
144 East Broadway

FUJIAN NOODLE HOUSES often have a range of meats to pick from to flavor and top your noodles, from beef to lamb to roast duck. The dish is then served to you in piping hot beef broth. Other spots to try include Super Taste at 26 Eldridge Street, Sheng Wang at 27 Eldridge Street, and Eastern Noodles at 28 Forsyth Street.

FU ZHOW RESTAURANT
137 East Broadway

EAST BROADWAY RESTAURANTS that cater to the new-immigrant clientele have some of the best prices in Chinatown. A complete meal can be had for $3.

YUN SUNG SEAFOOD RETAURANT
47 East Broadway

ANOTHER OF THE LARGER seafood restaurants in "Little Fuzhou," as the Fujian area around East Broadway, east of Bowery, is often called.

YOUNG CITY FISH BALLS
21 A Eldridge Street

THE FISH BALLS are the way to go at this establishment, but a word of warning if you're not a meat eater—Fujian fish balls are stuffed with ground pork.

TOP & MIDDLE: The cook at Nam Zhou stretches and flips the noodles to your desired thickness. You then pick your meat. BOTTOM: Fu Chow sauce for sale along East Broadway.

潮州、北京、四川

Teo Chew (Chiuchow), Beijing, Szechuan

BO KY, *80 Bayard Street*

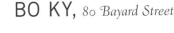

TOP: Owner Angle Ngo outside Bo Ky. LEFT: A staff member carves duck in the window of Bo Ky. NEXT PAGE: Outside Peking Duck House, 28 Mott Street.

ANGLE NGO is second generation Chinese Vietnamese. He speaks the Chinese Teo Chew dialect, Cantonese, Mandarin, Vietnamese, English, and even some Thai. "After Vietnam became communist in 1978, we escaped—we were the boat people, escaping to Thailand—and stayed there one year." His father had been a chef in an army garrison in Vietnam at the time of the escape. "We had a tough time staying in a communist country because after all we were a middle-class family, and the new regime wanted to relocate the city people to the farms, to create an all-new economical zone. My grandfather had been a businessman in Saigon City for many decades—suddenly you ask someone to become a farmer, it's a very tough life. So, obviously that's why we decided to leave the country."

His aunt, already in the United States, sponsored the family. For the first ten years the six kids went to school, and they all worked in Chinatown, selling food, his father at a fish market. Angle remembers selling vegetables on weekends to earn his allowance—and actively staying out of trouble, explaining, "There was a lot of gang activity; in the early eighties if you were fifteen or seventeen, walking down the wrong street could be dangerous." By 1988 they were able to start a small family business, in the form of Bo Ky.

All the recipes for Bo Ky came from his father. They have had the same secret formula for their slow-cooked beef and chicken broths since they opened almost twenty years ago. And once the deep, rich, beef broth has you under its spell, don't bother to press for those secrets—just know it's from scratch and includes five-spice powder and "something special." Angle says they rely a lot on locals for business, but have their share of tourists." At first people come in here asking for fried rice. I reply, 'I don't have that,' and they say, 'What kind of Chinese restaurant is this?' He says he thinks theirs is the only Chinese restaurant in Chinatown not serving fried rice.

"Everything is controlled by a family member, from the noodle broth to the condiments," says Angle. Specialty condiments, staples in Teo Chew cuisine, are chili hot sauce and a spicy chile marinated in vinegar.

"You can mix the sauces," Angle encourages, "It's like a cup of coffee, do you like cream, sugar, how much—it depends on the customer."

Signature dishes include seafood flat noodles, shrimp rolls, beef balls, and a uniquely potent curry chicken vermicelli with skinny rice noodles. Family-style Teo Chew options include flat noodles with pork, kidney and liver in soup as well as fish dumpling, which are essentially fish blended with flour, rolled, and stuffed with pork. Most items can come with the soup on the side, Southeast Asian style.

Country-style duck, which is boiled with cinnamon and soy sauce in a spiced broth (another secret), is one of the most popular items on the menu. They sell 110 ducks a day, 160 on weekends. He has one customer who comes in every week to buy six at once (he never asks why, but one imagines a chef uptown secretly slipping the aromatic, tender meat and crispy skin into his dishes).

While the cuisine of northern China, particularly Shandong, is not well represented in New York, one of its most famous dishes is Peking Duck, hailing, of course, from Beijing. Some Chinese restaurants in New York claim to serve this treasured dish, when really all they're doing is taking Cantonese roast duck and deep frying it just before serving to separate the meat from the skin. Real Peking Duck is a long process with several steps, including air drying the duck and blowing air underneath the skin before cooking. You eat the crispy skin first with flat, pancake-like buns folded with scallions and bean paste, then the meat is served sautéed. Traditionally, you would be served a milky soup made from the bones.

For another Peking duck option, try The Nice Restaurant at 35 East Broadway.

Fiery Szechuan cooking is yet another underrepresented cuisine in New York's Chinatown, but you can often find the dishes on Cantonese menus. Typical dishes of the region include kung pao chicken, dan-dan noodles in their spicy sesame sauce, wontons in red oil, and delicately crunchy twice-cooked pork. An exception to the normal spiciness is tea-smoked duck, a common Szechuan banquet dish. For Szechuan in Chinatown, stop by Grand Sichuan at 125 Canal Street.

SOUTHEAST ASIAN 東南亞

JAYA MALAYSIAN, *90 Baxter Street*

IN THE LAST TEN OR FIFTEEN YEARS, more Thai, Vietnamese, and Malaysian restaurants have sprung up in Chinatown, some opened by new immigrants who are ethnically Chinese but immigrated from Southeast Asia. Hann Low, proprietor of Jaya Malaysian, was part of one such family.

Hann says he grew up in the restaurant business. "It's got to be in the blood, it's a tough business." Living above his parents' coffee shop in Malaysia, he did some cooking at a young age, and got a basic understanding of how to handle the food. Joining his father, who had come the year before, Hann arrived in the States at nineteen and started working for his uncle, who had come many years before from Hong Kong, at his Chinese take-out restaurant. A year or two later, Hann's whole family arrived, one younger brother and four sisters.

The whole family decided to work together in the restaurant business. The first restaurant was a Chinese take-out place, and he went on to open three of the first (if not the first) Japanese restaurants in Brooklyn, named Fujisan. An American bar and grill was next, then he had an Italian restaurant for ten years. When more competition developed for the pasta place around 1993, Hann decided to open the first Thai restaurant in Brooklyn called the Lemongrass Grill, which subsequently took off. The second one opened in Manhattan in 1994 on upper Broadway, and he has six Lemongrass around Manhattan now. In 1996 he went back to Japanese, so many years later, and opened the upscale Sushihana at Seventy-eighth Street and Second Avenue. In the mean-

time, he had opened two Peruvian restaurants, one on Avenue A and one in Brooklyn.

"I go with what's popular, the trends, what the neighborhood needs. It's all about the food. The only way to keep my interest up is to try something new." He travels, reads widely and follows trends very closely. He says, "Whatever type of cuisine, you can tackle it as long as you know what kind of spices to use."

There were already some Malaysian restaurants in Chinatown by the time he opened Jaya in the mid-nineties, but watching the neighborhood over time he believed that it could support more. "Over the years, there are more people who know Malaysia. People have been traveling, they go to Singapore, to Thailand, and to Malaysia, it's a must." September 11 definitely hurt his business but promotions for Chinatown have helped, including the nearby Explore Chinatown information kiosk. Today 40 percent of his customers are tourists.

While the most well-known Malaysian dish is satay, Malaysian food actually embraces a diverse number of cuisines, including Malay, Indian, Thai, Chinese, and Indonesian. But, Hann emphasizes, this is not fusion food—you simply have distinct dishes that typically appear together on a menu in Malaysia. Curries and coconut, peanut pastes and spicy sauces typify the offerings, rounded out with beef, seafood, chicken, rice, and noodles. On the following pages, Hann Low shares recipes from his restaurant that reflect Malaysian as well as his Malaysian Chinese background. He has a penchant for Malaysian street food, reflected here as well as on his menu.

CHAR KWAY TEOW, STIR-FRIED BROAD RICE NOODLES

Adapted from a recipe courtesy of Jaya Malaysian Restaurant

This is a good example of Malaysian-Chinese roadside fast food. Once the noodles are cooked, the dish can be put together in a matter of minutes.

Makes 4 to 6 servings

Ingredients:

2 tablespoons vegetable oil

2 cloves garlic, minced

2 Chinese dried sausages, about 6 ounces, cut into ¼-inch thick diagonal slices

¼ pound small shrimp, peeled and deveined

2 tablespoons dark soy sauce

1 tablespoon light soy sauce

1 pound fresh broad rice noodles or ½ pound dried rice noodles, cooked according to package directions

⅔ cup sliced garlic chives, cut into 1½-inch pieces

1 cup bean sprouts, rinsed and drained

Directions:

1. In a wok set over medium-high heat, heat the oil until hot but not smoking. Add the garlic and stir-fry 30 seconds, until fragrant. Add the sausages and shrimp and stir-fry 1 minute. Add the dark and light soy sauce and the noodles and toss the ingredients until noodles are heated through. Add two-thirds of the garlic chives and bean sprouts and toss until combined well.

2. Transfer the mixture to a serving dish and garnish with the remaining garlic chives and bean sprouts.

BEEF *RENDANG*
(BEEF BRAISED IN COCONUT MILK)

Adapted from a recipe courtesy of Jaya Malaysian Restaurant

This is a wonderfully aromatic curry scented with the flavors of lemongrass and fresh ginger.

Makes 4 to 6 servings

For the Spice Paste Ingredients:

2 stalks lemongrass, green parts and hard outer leaves removed, chopped

A 1-inch piece fresh galangal, peeled and chopped, or 1½-inch piece fresh ginger, peeled and chopped

A 1-inch piece fresh ginger, peeled and chopped

3 cloves garlic, chopped

2 to 5 dried red chilis, according to the desired level of spiciness, seeds and stems discarded

1 tablespoon vegetable oil

For Beef Ingredients:

2 tablespoons vegetable oil

1 cup minced onion

1¼ to 1½ pounds flank steak, cut into 1½-inch cubes

1 to 2 tablespoons Malaysian or imported curry powder

2 turmeric leaves or 2 teaspoons ground turmeric

2 cups canned coconut milk

2 tablespoons thick soy sauce, or regular if not available

2 teaspoons sugar, or to taste

1 teaspoon salt, or to taste

Sliced cucumber and tomato for garnish

Directions:

1. Make the spice paste: In a food processor or blender combine all the ingredients and pulse until pureed. In a bowl, combine the steak cubes and the spice paste, stirring to coat.

2. In a wok or deep pan over medium-high heat, heat the oil until hot but not smoking. Add the onions and cook, stirring frequently, until golden brown, about 5 minutes. Add the meat and cook, stirring frequently, until no longer pink, about 10 minutes. Add the curry powder and turmeric leaves or ground turmeric, toss, and cook 1 minute. Add the coconut milk, soy sauce, sugar, and salt, bring to a boil and simmer, stirring occasionally, until the meat is tender and the sauce has thickened and reduced, 30 to 45 minutes.

3. Transfer the mixture to a serving dish and garnish with cucumber and tomato.

LAKSA NOODLES

Adapted from a recipe courtesy of Jaya Malaysian Restaurant

Another example of Malaysian-Chinese roadside fast food.

Makes 6 servings

For the Spice Paste Ingredients:

3 stalks lemongrass, green parts and hard outer leaves removed, chopped

A 2-inch piece galangal, peeled and chopped, or a 3-inch piece fresh ginger, peeled and chopped

A 2-inch piece fresh ginger, peeled and chopped

3 cloves garlic, chopped

1 tablespoon chili powder, or to taste

A 1-inch piece dry shrimp paste, or to taste

2 teaspoons ground coriander

1 teaspoon ground fennel

1 teaspoon ground cumin,

1 teaspoon ground turmeric

1 tablespoon vegetable oil

For the Noodle Soup Ingredients:

2 tablespoons vegetable oil

1 teaspoon imported curry powder

4 cups chicken stock or canned chicken broth

3 cups canned coconut milk

Salt and pepper to taste

1 pound small shrimp, peeled and deveined

12 ounces dried thin rice noodles or egg noodles

½ pound cooked skinless, boneless chicken breast, cut into 1-inch cubes

Fresh mint leaves, bean sprouts, and lime wedges for garnish

Directions:

1. Make the spice paste: In a food processor combine all the ingredients and process until pureed.

2. In a wide, deep pot set over medium-high heat, heat the oil until hot but not smoking. Add the spice paste and cook, stirring, for 2 minutes, or until very fragrant. Add the curry powder and cook, stirring, 1 minute. Add the stock and simmer over medium-low heat for 15 minutes. Add the coconut milk and salt and pepper to taste, and bring the soup to a simmer. Add the shrimp, and cook until the shrimp are opaque.

3. Meanwhile, cook the noodles according to the package directions. Drain the noodles and divide them among serving bowls. Ladle the soup over the noodles and top with the chicken, mint, bean sprouts, and lime wedges.

MORE SOUTHEAST ASIAN PICKS IN THE NEIGHBORHOOD

SANUR RESTAURANT
(Malaysian and some Indonesian), *18 Doyers Street*

THÁI SON VIETNAMESE, *89 Baxter Street*

THAILAND RESTAURANT, *106 Bayard Street*

SINGAPORE CAFÉ, *69 Mott Street*

融合菜式

FUSION

ALMOND FLOWER BISTRO, *96 Bowery*

WHEN VETERAN RESTAURATEUR and Chinatown native Sam Wong and chef Chris Chung, of Jean Georges, JUdson Grill, and Nobu training, set out to open Almond Flower in 2006, thcir inspiration was to elevate the dining experience in Chinatown. They wanted to bring world-class New American bistro food to the neighborhood in a comfortable, stylish atmosphere. It was a gamble. Even with the backing of three of the most successful businessmen in Chinatown, the test would be how a neighborhood conditioned to low prices, huge portions, and family-style dining would respond.

In preparation, Sam took some precautions on both sides of the fence. He eschewed candles on the tables, as they're associated with funerals in the Chinese community, and added two flat screen televisions, as Asians like them, but he refused to put chopsticks on the table and insisted that meals be served in Western-style courses, one after the other. Within weeks it became obvious that the neighborhood was ready to give Almond Flower a go. Office workers flocked in large groups (another Chinatown tradition, tough for a bistro kitchen to deal with), and lines went out the door Thursday through Saturday. Almond Flower has become a power-lunch spot for wealthy entrepreneurs from mainland China, and attracts the uptown crowd.

(See pages 47–53 for more on Sam Wong.)

TOP: Lobster tacos. MIDDLE: Calamari scented with cardamom salt. PREVIOUS PAGE: Braised beef lollipops: fried wontons stuffed with chopped braised short ribs.

Dishes include massaman duck with sweet potato croquettes, crispy spaghetti with mozzarella meatballs, and a lychee tart.

Since the infusion of Hong Kong immigrants in the 1980s, Hong Kong-style coffeehouses have sprung up as casual dining spots, popular with younger crowds. The fusion menus range from Cantonese snacks to satays, Japanese barbecued eel, and tuna fish toasts—there's even Spam on the menu at M Star. It's a humorous, marvelous clashing and mixing of cultures with options for any time of day. Try these spots out for a quick congee, fried chicken, or condensed milk toast and you'll appreciate the absurd, and quite well-prepared, variety.

MORE FUSION IN CHINATOWN

XO CAFÉ, *48 Hester Street, 96 Walker Street*

M STAR CAFÉ, *19 Division Street*

GREEN TEA CAFÉ, *45 Mott Street*

BAKERIES AND SWEETS 糕餅與甜點

CHINESE BAKERIES ARE SCATTERED throughout Chinatown. These establishments, both the older ones and newer Hong Kong-style versions, are places where tea or coffee and sweet or savory treats are enjoyed throughout the day, much like dim sum. In fact, there is some overlap in the offerings, such as steamed or roast pork or chicken buns. For the most part, however, the sweet selections are the focal points, and they come in a huge assortment, from coconut to cream-filled to strawberry or red bean. Classics include yellow, creamy egg custard tarts; chewy red bean paste buns; crunchy almond cookies; and glutinous sesame balls filled with bean paste. Also available are sponge cakes, flavored roll cakes, and slices of chocolate mousse or cheesecake. An appealing quality overall at these bakeries is the fact that most of the Chinese sweets are not overly sweet.

WHITE SWAN BAKERY, 24 Bowery

WHITE SWAN BAKERY is one of the older-style establishments, a popular place to come and read a newspaper or buy a moon cake to celebrate the Mid-Autumn Moon Festival.

MORE BAKERIES TO TRY

FAY DA BAKERY
*83 Mott Street, 191 Centre Street,
214-216 Grand Street*

MANNA HOUSE BAKERY
212 Grand Street, 125 Mott Street, 87 East Broadway

MARIA'S BAKERY, 42 Mott Street

EGG CUSTARD KING CAFÉ, 76 Mott Street

1. Birthday cakes and cake rolls. 2. As is customary in Chinatown bakeries, after you point out your desired items, a uniformed server will then compile your order off the shelves of savory and sweet baked goods. 3. Various Chinese buns. 4. Egg custard tarts sit next to baked roast pork buns.

CHINATOWN ICE CREAM FACTORY
65 Bayard Street. Christine and Philip Seid

TOP: Christine and Philip. The "exotic" ice creams on the menu board are American flavors, such as Oreo, chocolate caramel, and cherry vanilla, whereas the "regular" flavors include Asian favorites like lychee, durian, black sesame, and wasabi. BOTTOM: Brown candy sugar sold loose and packaged at Po Wing Hong.

PHILIP SEID GREW UP in and around Chinatown, at a time when the neighborhood was much smaller and ice cream was considered a bit of a luxury to most of its inhabitants. His grandparents were here already when his mother immigrated in 1948, and he was born in 1949. While his mother raised the four boys, his father worked as a restaurant worker, a shopkeeper, and in real estate. "It was a different time," remembers Philip with a smile. "Hot dogs were five cents."

When Philip and his brothers first opened the Chinatown Ice Cream Factory in 1978, their concept was to be a more welcoming, bilingual, and culturally sensitive shop than the average Häagen-Dazs or Carvel options that were the norm. This translates to their flavors as well, which range from lychee and durian to Oreo and vanilla. It wasn't easy in the then very conservative Chinese community, Philip remembers. "We were pioneers. People would laugh and ask, 'Why don't you open a restaurant?'" Christine, Philip's daughter, agrees, pointing out that they were bringing two cultures together. "For example," she says, "Chinese cultural tradition dictates that you're not supposed to eat cold foods in the winter. It took a while to catch on," she says, "but the lines are out the door these days. Manhattan has changed. Now you see older Chinese people buying our ice cream and that's one of the most flattering things."

The ice cream at the factory—a sliver of a store on Bayard—is ultra-premium, rich, and smooth, and does not skimp on ingredients. "We like it to stay small; it's nice to be in the neighborhood. We know our neighbors here, we don't know them in Queens." Happy to keep the family business going, Christine continues, "Chinatown is a center for Chinese people to meet. You can't walk down the street without knowing people. It's a homey feeling." She has worked at the store since she was a child, and credits the work with teaching her how to save her own money and stay out of trouble.

They have no delivery system, but that doesn't deter people from picking up to-order ice cream cakes. In fact, one man used two cakes to propose to his fiancée (*Will you marry me?* on one and her name on the other) . . . in Canada! ○

RED BEAN ICE CREAM

Adopted from a recipe courtesy of the Chinatown Ice Cream Factory

This recipe has at its core a red bean soup recipe Christine's grandmother used to make.

Makes 3 cups red bean paste. Makes 1½ quarts ice cream

Red Bean Paste Ingredients (see note):
A 12-ounce package Chinese red beans
A cinnamon stick (optional)
¼ cup granulated sugar
1 stick Chinese candy sugar, broken into small pieces

Ice Cream Ingredients:
1½ cups whole milk
1 cup plus 2 tablespoons granulated sugar
3 cups heavy cream
1 tablespoon pure vanilla extract
Red food coloring, if desired

Directions:

1. Make the red bean paste: Rinse the beans in a colander. Transfer them to a bowl, and cover with cold water. Soak overnight.

2. Drain the beans, place in a 3-quart saucepan, and add 6 cups water. Add the cinnamon stick, if desired. Bring to a boil over medium-high heat, lower the heat and simmer 2½ hours, or until beans are very tender. Check the pan frequently to make sure the water hasn't been completely absorbed before the beans are cooked and replenish as necessary.

3. Drain the beans and discard the cinnamon stick. Add the granulated sugar and stir to dissolve. Add the Chinese candy sugar and stir to dissolve. Place the beans in a food processor and process until smooth. Transfer to a container and chill, covered, until ready to use.

4. In a bowl, whisk together the milk, sugar, cream, and vanilla until the sugar is dissolved. Stir in ½ cup of the red bean paste, or to taste, and a drop of red food coloring, if desired. Freeze the mixture in an ice cream machine according to the manufacturer's instructions.

Note: **Although homemade red bean paste is preferable if time permits, canned red bean paste is a good substitute in this recipe. Christine suggests using the extra bean paste as a filling for pastries or layer cake, or as a topping for waffles. You can freeze the paste, but it is best to use it fresh as it has a tendency to get a little bit watery when frozen.**

Celebration

New Year's visit in Chinatown, circa 1912.

節慶

不可或缺的節慶

CELEBRATIONS ARE INTEGRAL to Chinese tradition, and banquets are always at their center in Chinatown. Banquet halls are sprinkled throughout the neighborhood, designed to accommodate the large variety of feasts and the endless reasons families come up with to have them—from weddings to job promotions to annual festivals and family gatherings.

From the measured rules of Confucius to the mandated banqueting of the Ming, Manchu, and Ch'ing dynasties, where one was served dozens of dishes in one sitting, feasts are laden with ritual and symbolism. Today the average banquet contains ten courses, but it could be eight or twelve. Regardless, it is always an even number, excluding the rice course.

Weddings in Chinatown are elaborate affairs. The bride changes up to five or seven times, transitioning from the American white to the elaborate traditional red formal wear to evening gowns. And the feast is punctuated by several different performers throughout the meal. At one such affair at Jing Fong, the following ten-course menu was served to more than 500 guests:

1. A platter of seaweed salad, Hokkai clams, duck tongue, fried pork strips, and jellyfish
2. Scallops and Chinese broccoli
3. Sea cucumber and abalone
4. Lobster stuffed with scallions and ginger
5. Steamed whole fish
6. Roast squab
7. Steamed shrimp
8. Fried rice and pan-fried noodles
9. Shark's fin soup
10. Oranges, sesame balls, gelatin squares, and cake

LEFT: Streamers fall through the sky above Mott Street. Traditionally, rather than streamers you'd see fireworks going off throughout the parade—loud noises meant to ward off the dragon—but they were banned by the city for safety reasons, and are centralized now, ignited by officials in the center of Chatham Square.

祥龍獻瑞 A dragon chasing a pearl, representing the sun, is shimmied down East Broadway by a group of dancers. Though generally the dragon is a very benevolent, imperial, mythical symbol in China, one legend exists wherein a dragon was repeatedly terrorizing a village. The story goes that the villagers were able to fend him off using fire, loud noises, and the color red, which he feared. Each year the dragon comes back and the ritual must be repeated. Everyone waits in anticipation to see the longest dragon of the parade.

Served in succession, the dishes are meant to flow easily one into the other on your palate. For example, a spicy dish is not served directly before or after a mild dish. There is a transition in terms of richness and heat that generally peaks in the middle of the banquet then gently flows toward the soothing rice and delicate shark's fin. Serving such a huge amount to so many, the dozens of waiters and waitresses at Jing Fong spun and swirled across the room in constant motion, stacking new plates, serving guests and, in an unique Chinatown twist, providing take-out containers so that guests could take home food they had not finished at night's end. The tables were spread with red cloths, as red is the traditional color for weddings, symbolizing good luck, happiness, and celebration. Each table in the room was set for ten people, in the classic banquet ratio of ten dishes for ten guests.

The dragon and phoenix are prominently displayed along the wall at all banquet halls and many other Chinatown restaurants, as they might host smaller wedding banquets. The dragon represents the groom, while the phoenix represents the bride. Foods are also given this association; lobster or shrimp is served as the "dragon" and chicken or squab as the "phoenix." The bride and groom's traditional clothing is often embroidered with the symbols. Many of the dishes served at a wedding banquet hold some symbolic meaning; shark's fin (a delicacy) is served for prosperity, and whole fish is served for abundance and togetherness. Tables are strewn with melon seeds to represent the many hoped-for children.

NOTABLE CHINATOWN BANQUET HALLS INCLUDE

JING FONG, *20 Elizabeth Street*

GOLDEN BRIDGE, *50 Bowery*

GOLDEN UNICORN, *18 East Broadway*

GRAND HARMONY, *98 Mott Street*

ORIENTAL PEARL, *103-105 Mott Street*

LEFT: The grand entrance to Jing Fong features a chandelier and escalator. MIDDLE: The back wall and stage area at Golden Unicorn. RIGHT: Jing Fong's banquet room is the largest in Chinatown, seating 1,000 guests. OPPOSITE: Another brilliantly dressed Beijing opera character turns down East Broadway at Chatham Square.

A lion dance troupe winds its way down the streets, bowing to each establishment to ensure a prosperous New Year. As they go, they collect red envelopes called Hang Bao (or Lai-See) of "lucky money" for the performers as well as community and charity groups. It is believed that if you "feed" the lion an envelope you will be protected and have good fortune in the coming year. Restaurants also set out lettuce, representing money, for the lion to eat. Accompanying the lion dancers (it takes two people, one for the front and one for the back) are a group of musicians, playing drums, cymbals, and a gong. A smiling monk or buddha in a pink mask walks beside the lion as his master. By waving his fan he "tames" and guides the lion, who can often become playful with the crowd while making his rounds. Most lion dancers in Chinatown are "southern" lions, linked to the martial arts from that region. Lion dancing is performed by martial arts troupes as well as designated lion dance troupes. Northern Chinese lions, on the other hand, are often seen in Chinese acrobatic performances, sporting shaggy, long hair and smaller heads.

THE LUNAR NEW YEAR

BY FAR THE LARGEST CELEBRATION in China and Chinatown is the Lunar New Year, also known as the Spring Festival. Following the lunar calendar, it takes place over two weeks, usually starting in January or February, and ends on the full moon. Chinatown celebrates this festival, honoring family and new beginnings, with a folk arts festival, flower market, and its largest parade of the year, featuring everything from school bands to Chinese opera characters and martial artists, as well as the stars of the show: lions and dragons.

FROM TOP LEFT: 1. In Chinese fables, there are three popular figures, called Star Gods, that represent good fortune (Fu), wealth (Lu) and longevity (Shou). Often you see them on New Year's cards. Depicted here is most likely the deity for good fortune, Fu. **2.** A small lion's head peers above the packed streets and sidewalks at the old Chinatown nexus of Mott, Bayard, and Pell Streets. **3.** The man dressed in yellow and red is depicting an emperor of the Qing dynasty. To his left is a character from the Beijing opera in traditional full rich costume and makeup. **4.** Martial arts are performed all along the parade route, students and masters beautifully choreographed in unison. This man is from Shao Lin Temple in Flushing, Queens. **5.** A fierce dragon takes to the streets. **6.** The arrival of the longest dragon. **7.** Dancing and drumming in festive dress, groups often parade together to represent different provinces in China. **8.** 2006 was the Year of the Dog, and New York dog lovers came out in full regalia. Each year follows the Chinese zodiacal calendar, symbolized by one of twelve animals, such as the rat, the snake, or the rooster, with different characteristics. People born in that year are said to share those traits. **9.** The Lantern Festival is celebrated on the last day of the Lunar New Year. Lanterns are lit in abundance, officially welcoming spring. Some say they symbolize the fire that drove the dragon away, but yet another legend is of Dongfang, an imperial minister who predicted the burning of a village. The Jade Emperor himself had ordered the Fire Goddess to burn the village, and while sympathetic to the village, she must carry out the order. Dongfang devised a successful plan: the villagers made the Fire Goddess's favorite sweet rice dumplings to appease her, and everyone lit lanterns, fireworks, and bonfires to fool the Jade Emperor into thinking his order had been followed. **10.** Another proud owner celebrates the Year of the Dog.

年的饗宴

A Lunar New Year Banquet

OPPOSITE: A Chinatown Lunar New Year's greeting, circa 1912. Though it might look like they're holding teacups, the two men are probably toasting with liquor from one of the bottles on the table. TOP: On the table are traditional food symbols for New Year's, such as round fruit to recall the moon, and the octagonal "Tray of Togetherness," filled with dried fruit and nuts.

EIGHT COURSES, NOT INCLUDING RICE, are considered a positive number for a Lunar New Year banquet, as the word for eight sounds like "grow." Many Chinese traditions have at their root a homonym, the sound of a character sounding like another Chinese word and thus taking on meaning. Nowhere is this more apparent than at a banquet table, particularly a Lunar New Year feast, as it is believed that what you eat will affect the coming year.

Nian gao, steamed sticky rice cakes often sweetened with dates and brown sugar, is one such food eaten during the holiday. The word *gao* sounds like the word for higher, thus by eating it you can be expected to advance in the New Year. They are generally bought in Chinatown at a bakery. Taro root cakes are eaten as symbols of rising fortune and prosperity. Given in pairs, tangerines are favored as the word for them, *gut jai*, sounds like luck, and they resemble gold, symbolizing wealth. In the tradition of northern China, *jiao zi*, pork dumplings with Napa cabbage and garlic chives, are eaten as they resemble gold coins for prosperity.

An eight-sided tray symbolizing family togetherness and consisting of dried fruit or candy—each with their own symbolic good fortune—is traditionally set out for visitors, with melon seeds for fertility and wealth placed in the center. These trays can be bought prepackaged in Chinatown groceries.

Nearly all foods eaten during the holiday carry meaning. Below are a selection of recipes and their symbolic purpose at a banquet, courtesy of Eric Tsang, the manager of Fuleen Seafood restaurant on Division Street, should you wish to create a banquet of your own. Very few Chinatown families still create their own banquets at home, but many of the restaurants, such as Fuleen, Mandarin Court, Ping's and Golden Unicorn, serve special Lunar New Year menus.

SHARK'S FIN SOUP

Adapted from a recipe courtesy of
Fuleen Seafood Restaurant

A symbol of prosperity, no banquet is complete without it. If you are vegetarian, or are opposed to the use of shark's fin, mung bean vermicelli (cellophane noodles) are a common and good substitute. In fact, they are often used in place of shark's fin to cut costs at large banquets, and can be found as a cheaper option on some Chinatown menus. In this recipe, 4 ounces of mung bean vermicelli, which have been soaked in warm water for 15 minutes or until soft, can be added to the soup just before serving.

Makes 4 servings

Ingredients:

1 block dried shark's fin, about 7 to 8 ounces
6 cups chicken stock or canned broth
1 tablespoon Chinese white vinegar or white distilled vinegar
1 tablespoon Shao Hsing wine, sake, or dry Sherry
1 tablespoon Chinese oyster sauce
½ teaspoon salt
¼ teaspoon ground white pepper
1 tablespoon minced fresh ginger
3 tablespoons minced scallion
½ cup cooked crabmeat
2 tablespoons cornstarch dissolved in ¼ cup water
1 to 2 teaspoons sesame oil, or to taste

Directions:

1. In a bowl, combine the shark's fin with enough cold water to cover and soak for 3 hours, or until softened. Drain the shark's fin in a fine strainer, being careful not to lose any of the strands.

2. Transfer the shark's fin to a heatproof dish. In a bowl combine 1 cup water, the vinegar and wine, and pour it over the shark's fin. Place the dish in a steamer and steam, covered, 30 minutes. Carefully drain the shark's fin in a fine sieve and rinse under cold water.

3. In a saucepan set over medium heat, combine the shark's fin, stock, oyster sauce, salt, and white pepper and simmer, partially covered, 20 minutes. Add the ginger, scallion, and crabmeat and simmer 10 minutes more. Stir the cornstarch mixture, add it to the broth, and simmer, stirring, until lightly thickened. Season with sesame oil to taste.

MONK'S DISH *OR* JAI

Adapted from a recipe courtesy of
Fuleen Seafood Restaurant

Oysters are eaten as a symbol for luck in business, while fat choy (a hairlike seaweed) is a symbol for prosperity. Fat choy ho si is translated as greetings and well wishes for someone to become rich. While there are exceptions, such as the recipe below, frequently Jai or monk's dish is strictly vegetarian if served on the first day of the New Year—the hope being that by not eating meat or anything that has been killed you can both counteract excess of the night before, and attract good karma. The dried oysters are very strong in flavor, even after all of the processes the recipe takes them through definitely an acquired taste. Only top-quality dried oysters should be used.

Makes 4 to 6 servings

Ingredients:

½ pound dried oysters (about 12)

1 quart peanut oil for deep frying

1 tablespoon peanut oil

2 cloves garlic, minced

1 tablespoon minced fresh ginger

½ cup minced red onion

1 cup chicken broth

2 tablespoons Shao Hsing wine, sake, or dry Sherry

1 tablespoon Chu Hou sauce, or hoisin if not available (see page 211 for Resources)

1 tablespoon oyster sauce

1 teaspoon sugar

¼ cup soaked and drained dry black moss (fat choy seaweed)

1 teaspoon cornstarch dissolved in 3 tablespoons water

Directions:

1. In a bowl, combine the oysters with enough cold water to cover by 1 inch and soak overnight. Drain the oysters and squeeze dry.

2. In a heavy saucepan or deep-fat fryer, heat the quart of peanut oil to 320°F. Add the oysters and fry until crisp. With a slotted spoon, transfer the oysters to a plate lined with paper towels to drain. Arrange the oysters in one layer in a heatproof dish. Place the dish in a steamer or a pot fitted with a small inverted bowl or ramekin upon which you can place the dish above but not touching a couple of inches of water. Cover the pot and steam, replacing water that has evaporated as needed, for 1 hour.

3. In a wok or saucepan set over medium heat, heat the peanut oil until hot but not smoking. Add the garlic and ginger and cook, stirring, 30 seconds. Add the onion and cook, stirring, 2 minutes. Add the chicken broth, wine, Chou Hou sauce, oyster sauce, sugar, and oysters. Simmer 20 minutes.

4. Add the black moss to the pan, carefully pulling the strands apart to separate them, laying them on top of the oysters and gently stirring to distribute. Stir the cornstarch mixture and add it to the pan. Cook, stirring, until sauce is lightly thickened. The dish can be served with the black moss plated in a ring around the oysters.

SNAILS IN BLACK BEAN SAUCE

Adapted from a recipe courtesy of
Fuleen Seafood Restaurant

These are really more of an appetizer, as you don't get much meat out of each snail. If you can, try to get them pre-cracked and cooked, to lighten the process.

Makes 2 servings

Ingredients:

1 pound snails (in their shells) soaked in cold water for 3 hours, drained, and rinsed

2 tablespoons fermented black beans (not in sauce)

½ cup chicken broth

1 tablespoon Shao Hsing wine, sake, or dry Sherry

1 tablespoon light soy sauce

½ teaspoon cornstarch

1 tablespoon peanut oil

1 tablespoon minced garlic

1 tablespoon minced fresh ginger

1 tablespoon Chu Hou sauce, or hoisin if not available (see page 211 for Resources)

Directions:

1. In a saucepan over high heat, combine the snails with enough water to cover. Bring to a boil and simmer 20 minutes. Drain.

2. Rinse the black beans in several changes of cold water, drain, and pat dry. Mash the beans with the back of a spoon.

3. Make the sauce: In a bowl, combine all the broth, wine, soy sauce, and cornstarch.

4. In a wok set over medium-high heat, heat the oil until hot but not smoking. Add the garlic, ginger, and black beans and cook, stirring, 30 seconds, or until fragrant. Add the Chu Hou sauce and cook, stirring, 10 seconds. Add the snails and cook, stirring, 1 minute. Stir the sauce ingredients and add to the wok. Bring to a boil and simmer, stirring, 30 seconds more, or until lightly thickened.

BIRD'S NEST SOUP

This unique dish is served as a dessert, and is said to bring long life, youth, and beauty. Birds' nests are often given as gifts, and they can cost anywhere from $25 to $1,000 each. For this recipe you can use pieces of a bird's nest, if buying them whole proves too expensive. (See page 176 for more on this treasured item.)

Makes 4 servings

Ingredients:

½ cup loosely packed dried bird's nest

2 cups canned coconut milk

½ cup Chinese rock sugar (small crystals)

Directions:

1. Soak the bird's nest in warm water to cover overnight, or cover the nest with 3 cups boiling water and soak 4 hours. Drain.

2. Blanch the soaked bird's nest in boiling water 5 minutes. Drain.

3. In a saucepan over medium heat, combine the bird's nest, coconut milk, 1 cup water, and sugar. Simmer 30 minutes. Ladle into individual bowls.

STIR-FRIED CHINESE BROCCOLI

Adapted from a recipe courtesy of Fuleen Seafood Restaurant

Served whole, Chinese broccoli is a symbol for jade, which brings good health and youth. Chinese broccoli resembles Italian broccoli rabe but does not have its bitter flavor. Look for stalks that are deep green and firm. If the stalks are thick, they will need to be halved lengthwise for even cooking. Wash the broccoli in several changes of water, drain well, and pat dry with paper towel before cooking

Makes 4 servings

Ingredients:

1 tablespoon vegetable oil

1 tablespoon minced fresh ginger

2 cloves garlic, minced

¾ pound Chinese broccoli, rinsed, drained, stalk and leaves separated

3 tablespoons chicken broth

1 tablespoon Shao Hsing wine, sake, or dry Sherry

Directions:

In a wok over medium-high heat, heat the oil until hot but not smoking. Add the ginger and garlic and stir-fry 30 seconds. Add the broccoli stalks and stir-fry 1 minute. Add the leaves and stir-fry 1 minute more, or until bright green. Add the chicken broth and simmer 1 to 2 minutes, or until the liquid is almost completely evaporated and broccoli is firm yet tender. Add the wine and toss to coat.

STEAMED SEA BASS WITH GINGER AND SCALLIONS

**Adapted from a recipe courtesy of
Fuleen Seafood Restaurant**

The word for whole fish, yu, sounds like abundance, and serving it whole also symbolizes togetherness as well as reproduction.

Makes 2 servings

Fish Ingredients:

A 1¼- to 1½-pound sea bass, cleaned, rinsed, and patted dry

1 tablespoon Shao Hsing wine, sake, or dry Sherry

1 tablespoon light soy sauce

1 teaspoon sesame oil

¼ teaspoon salt

2 tablespoons julienned fresh ginger

2 tablespoons julienned scallion

4 sprigs fresh cilantro

Topping Ingredients:

2 tablespoons julienned fresh ginger

4 tablespoons julienned scallion

2 tablespoons peanut oil

Directions:

1. Lay the fish in a shallow, heatproof dish. In a small bowl combine the wine, soy sauce, sesame oil, and salt. Coat the fish inside and out with the mixture and place 1 tablespoon of the ginger in the cavity of fish. Place the remaining ginger and scallion and cilantro on top of the fish.

2. Transfer the dish to a steamer (or a large pot with a couple inches of water that has been fitted with an inverted bowl or ramekin upon which to place the dish above the water) and steam, covered, 15 minutes, or until a chopstick can be inserted easily into the fish.

3. Transfer the fish to a serving dish and top with julienned ginger and scallion. In a small saucepan set over medium heat, heat the oil until hot. Pour over fish and serve.

ABOVE: Hong Kong–style sea bass with ginger and scallions, just before steaming. OPPOSITE: As freshness is by far the most sought-after quality in Hong Kong–style seafood restaurants, Fuleen maintains tanks of live fish and shellfish in their front window and entry way.

LONGEVITY NOODLES
WITH CRABMEAT

**Adapted from a recipe courtesy of
Fuleen Seafood Restaurant**

Longevity noodles are eaten to symbolize a long life. Note that this style of noodle, packaged in rectangular cakes, is precooked and shouldn't be left in the water for too long before stir-frying.

Makes 4 servings

Ingredients:

One 8-ounce cake of yee mein or e-fu noodles

1 cup fish or chicken stock or canned chicken broth

2 tablespoons oyster sauce

1 to 2 teaspoons dark soy sauce

2 teaspoons cornstarch

1½ teaspoons sesame oil

¼ teaspoon salt

¼ teaspoon sugar

2 tablespoons peanut oil

1 tablespoon minced fresh ginger

1 tablespoon minced garlic

½ ounce dried black shiitake mushrooms, soaked, drained, and sliced (½ cup)

6 ounces crabmeat, picked over

1 bunch Chinese yellow leeks (chives) or scallions, white and pale green parts, cut into 1½-inch lengths (1½ cups)

Directions:

1. In a large pot of boiling salted water, add the noodles and cook, stirring to separate the noodles, according to package directions, about 5 minutes. Run cold water into the pot and drain. Rinse noodles with cold water and drain once again. Set aside.

2. Make the sauce: In a bowl combine the stock, oyster sauce, soy sauce, cornstarch, sesame oil, salt, and sugar.

3. In a wok set over medium-high heat, heat the peanut oil until hot but not smoking. Add the ginger and garlic and cook, stirring, 30 seconds, or until fragrant. Add the mushrooms and crab and cook, stirring, 1 minute. Add the leeks and toss to combine.

4. Stir the sauce ingredients, add to the wok, and bring to a simmer. Add the noodles and cook, stirring, until sauce is absorbed, 1 or 2 minutes. Transfer to a platter and serve.

2 tablespoons peanut oil

1 tablespoon Chinese white vinegar or distilled vinegar

1 tablespoon Shao Hsing wine, sake, or dry Sherry

2 teaspoons sesame oil

1 teaspoon sugar

½ teaspoon salt

Sauce Ingredients:

1 tablespoon peanut oil

4 tablespoons shredded fresh ginger

4 scallions, white and pale green parts, cut into julienne strips

2 cloves garlic, minced

1 tablespoon cornstarch dissolved in ⅔ cup chicken broth

2 teaspoons sesame oil

Directions:

1. Arrange the chicken in a shallow heatproof dish. In a bowl combine the ginger, scallions, peanut oil, vinegar, wine, sesame oil, sugar, and salt. Add the mixture to chicken and turn to coat the chicken with the seasonings. (Note: If you do not have a large enough pot or steamer you may cut into serving pieces prior to seasoning.)

2. Place the dish in a large steamer (or a large pot with a couple inches of water that is fitted with an inverted bowl upon which to place the dish), cover, and steam for 1 to 1½ hours (45 minutes if cut into serving pieces), or until the chicken is tender. Be sure to add boiling water to pan to replace water that has evaporated. Keep warm while preparing the sauce.

3. Make the sauce: In a wok or skillet set over medium-high heat, heat the oil until hot but not smoking. Add the ginger, scallions, and garlic and cook, stirring, 30 seconds, or until fragrant. Add the cornstarch mixture and simmer, stirring, until lightly thickened. Add the sesame oil. Pour the sauce over the chicken and serve sliced.

CHICKEN WITH GINGER AND SCALLIONS

Adapted from a recipe courtesy of
Fuleen Seafood Restaurant

Chicken also symbolizes prosperity. On the New Year's table it is often served whole, with feet and head intact, for a good start and finish for the year.

Makes 4 servings

Chicken Ingredients:

A 2½- to 3-pound chicken

2 tablespoons shredded fresh ginger

2 scallions, white and pale green parts, cut into julienne strips

ABOVE: Moon cakes sold at White Swan Bakery on the Bowery. Often the molds depict the Moon Goddess or the Jade Rabbit. Also available at this time are wheat or ginger cookies in shapes such as the Jade Rabbit, fish, crabs, and the God of Longevity.

THE MID-AUTUMN MOON FESTIVAL

THE MID-AUTUMN MOON, or Harvest Moon Festival, is celebrated at the mid-harvest full moon, the fifteenth day of the eighth month of the lunar calendar. The most important food tradition is to make or purchase a moon cake. Traditionally, revelers and families light candles in honor of their ancestors and serve the cake just as the moon reaches its brightest point. The legend associated with the festival has a few variations, but the essential story goes that Chang-E, the beautiful wife of an officer of the imperial guard, once took an immortality potion meant for her husband. She began to float and was thus transported to the moon as her husband chased her. Once there, she was turned into a three-legged frog in punishment. Her love for her husband did not die, however, and shines brightest on the harvest moon. She is called the Lady or Goddess of the Moon, and small children make wishes to her. Colorful pictures of symbols like the Moon Goddess and the Jade Rabbit—who is said to live on the moon with her, making immortality potions with a mortar and pestle—are displayed during this festival, and apples, persimmons, grapes, or melons are set out, all round like the moon.

Moon cakes are usually made in a mold and filled with a variety of ingredients. There are savory meat-filled or vegetable cakes as well as sweet, with a medley of dried fruits and nuts or lotus or red bean paste. Some cakes have an entire duck egg, symbolizing the moon, baked into the center.

Taro is also eaten during this festival, commemorating how Ming dynasty soldiers were saved from starvation during a battle after having found taro by the light of the autumn moon. And yet another dish popular at this time is snails in black bean sauce. The story behind the dish involves a resourceful Qing dynasty magistrate who orchestrated a truce between warring neighbors. In an attempt to ruin each other's crops, each continually dumped snails onto the other's land. The magistrate's elegant solution to bring them to their senses was to gather and cook up the snails and serve the feast under the autumn moon, in appreciation of the earth's fertility and abundance. ○

第四章 CHAPTER No. 04 肆

Tea in Chinatown

At Ten Ren they use Yi-Xing tea ware, which has been favored since the Ming dynasty (sixteenth century) for its beauty and ability to enhance the flavor and aroma of the tea. The fine purple clay is not glazed, and actually absorbs some of the tea when used, becoming seasoned over time and handed down through generations.

品茗

天仁茗茶

TEN REN TEA AND GINSENG CO., *75 Mott Street*

IN 1984 MARK AND ELLEN LII drove cross-country from San Francisco with their six-month-old son, arriving in New York on a mission: to introduce the region to the finest teas in the world. In our current time of green tea worship and antioxidant fervor, it may be hard to remember what a challenge that was more than two decades ago. Simply put, New Yorkers didn't have a taste for tea quite yet. In general, tea meant boxes of Lipton bags, or the occasional Bigelow herb infusion.

Mark's qualifications as an ambassador of tea run deep, however, and he was not thwarted. His ancestors came to Taiwan from China 200 years ago, making his the eighth generation in Taiwan. His great-grandfather started tea farming, and his great-uncle moved to the city of Kang Shan in 1954 to establish a tea business, in the form of the Ming Feng Tea Shop. In the sixties, the name of the company was changed to Ten Ren, which means "heavenly love" and "four persons," which was auspicious as at that point four brothers were involved. By 1978 they had fifteen stores in Taiwan. "I had just graduated from university, and my uncle wanted to expand his business to the U.S.," Mark recalls, "Seeing the influx of Asians immigrating to the U.S. in the sixties and seventies, he felt there was a large enough market to support a retail store. I came to Los Angeles July 4, 1980."

While getting his MBA at Claremont University, Mark and his wife Ellen trained in the Los Angeles store. By 1982 they opened a store in San Francisco with his uncle. New York was the next obvious choice, given its large Chinatown. "I took almost five months to find the store at 176 Canal Street, and spent a month renovating it," says Mark, "We opened in December 1984. We couldn't compare our business to anything here, because there were no other specialty tea stores. People said we would be closed in six months." Despite crushingly high rent, Mark and Ellen were determined to make it work. "On May 29, 1985, the *New*

TOP: Mark and Ellen Lii OPPOSITE: Mark's family plantation in Song Po Ling, Taiwan. The name means Pine Tree Hill. The elevation of the plantation is 1,300 to 1,600 feet.

York Times reviewed us, saying that we had brought tea from Taiwan to New York and it was more expensive than gold per pound." People were curious, and they had a boost in business and managed to survive.

In setting up their store, one of their requirements was that the staff be trained and wear uniforms. This set them apart from the rest of Chinatown, where businesses were traditionally run solely by family members. With the upscale feel, people were sometimes intimidated. "They come into the store and see the prices and stick out their tongues," explains Ellen. "At that time they could get 100 Lipton tea bags for a couple dollars. How are you going to explain? In this country they don't grow tea and they don't have any background in it. The only way is to educate. So we have free sample tastings every day. Each person who walks in the store gets a sample. Today there is a huge difference. Americans buy big canisters, and come in for Christmas gifts."

They've gone practically everywhere to promote and demonstrate the culture and fine art of tea: department stores, primary and middle schools, the New York Public Library, the Queens Botanical Garden, the Asia Society, the China Institute. They also teach tea classes in English and Chinese: More than 6,000 people have taken their tea class in Chinese, and more than 3,000 people have attended the English classes.

The Liis have continued to expand their business over the years. After a second Chinatown was formed in Flushing, they opened a store there in 1988. In 1992 they moved their flagship store from Canal to Mott Street, as it was the center of Chinatown tourism.

The next big boost to their business came in 1994. *The New England Journal of Medicine* published an article about green tea and cancer prevention. Mark remembers, "At that time, no one knew green tea, and it was very hard to find. Many, many media came to our store to interview us, Channel 7, even [radio station] WOR, and finally the *New York Times*. That article came out on a Wednesday and the next day more than 200 people came to my store to buy green tea. Two hundred thirty-four people came for English tea classes." He found himself teaching English tea classes nonstop for the next ten days. "Twelve years later, and now everybody knows this, and our sales volume increased. People consume green tea now without explanation."

In 1997 they opened their third store on Eighth Avenue in Brooklyn's Chinatown—again following the Chinese community. And finally, in 1998 bubble tea became popular, so they opened tea bars in 2001 on Mott street, in 2004 on Lafayette Street near SoHo, and in Elmhurst, Queens.

TOP: The interior of the flagship store on Mott Street.
BOTTOM: Loose tea is packed to order by a staff member.

Also sold at Ten Ren tea shops are copious amounts of fine ginseng. The Ten Ren company owns a 120-acre ginseng plantation in Wisconsin, growing cultivated as well as the more precious "woods grown" American ginseng in a nearby forest. (See page 177 for more on ginseng and its healing properties.)

Today, the Ten Ren company has almost sixty stores in North America and seventy-five in Taiwan. And since 1993, the company has opened more than 650 stores in mainland China under the name Ten Fu Tea. In Taiwan Ten Ren runs ten large tea-house restaurants, where dishes are flavored with tea. In the next few years, New Yorkers can look forward to Ten Ren Tea House arriving in Midtown.

茶的種類

TYPES OF TEAS

"WHEN I CAME IN 1980, my mission was to introduce the best tea in the world to the American people, oolong tea. Prior to 1994 jasmine tea and oolong tea were most popular with the customers. But the newspapers defeated me in 1994 with green tea," Mark says with a chuckle. "The second most popular now is semi-fermented tea. Light fermented tea we call oolong and Tekuan Yin, which means Iron Goddess of Mercy. Heavy fermented tea is Pu-erh tea, which is very popular in the Cantonese dim sum houses as it helps digest oily foods. Then comes black tea."

Below are a few of the teas featured at Ten Ren, by category, with the brewing methods that they recommend according to the properties and style of the tea leaves.

DRAGONWELL TEA: Note the unique flat sword shape. Grown in the West Lake region of China, the green leaves are hand picked in the early spring and delicately handled so as to prevent breakage. TO BREW: Heat the water so that it is not hot, not boiling, about 175°F. Use 2 teaspoons of tea per 6 ounces of water; steep 1 or 2 minutes. The leaves can be infused up to three times.

GUNPOWDER GREEN: True to its name, this tea is rolled into tiny pellets and has a hint of smokiness in its flavor. China exported this to South Africa for the nutritional value. It is also used paired with mint in Morocco. TO BREW: Bring the water to a boil and let it cool for 5 minutes. Use about 1 teaspoon of tea per 8 ounces of water. Let steep 3 to 5 minutes. The leaves can be infused a second time.

NON-FERMENTED GREEN TEA:

This category of tea is heat-blanched and dried in one process to immediately stop oxidation of the leaves. They are then twisted (if called for) and dried. Mark and Ellen recommend drinking green tea in the morning, as it gives you strength and "stirs you up."

SEMI-FERMENTED OOLONG TEA:

These teas are left to dry or "wither" in direct sunlight and then moved to a heated room to dry further and "ferment." Once they've reached the desired level of fermentation they are blanched to stop the process, twisted or rolled, and dried. The leaves are sifted, and the stalks are cut or extracted. The next process, called "wind selecting" at the Ten Ren factories, separates the main tea leaves from smaller pieces. Teas sold at Ten Ren come in up to five or six grades, the first being the finest and most expensive.

PEARL JASMINE: This is the finest variety of jasmine tea. The very young green buds are just slightly fermented, scented with jasmine petals, and manually rolled and twisted into a bowl shape the size of pearls. TO BREW: Bring fresh water to a boil; let it cool for 5 minutes. Use 1 teaspoon of tea per 8 ounces of water. Let steep for 3 to 5 minutes. The leaves can be infused a second time.

TUNG TIN GREEN OOLONG: Manually rolled in a semi-bowl shape, this highly prized tea has a fresh taste and an almost flowery fragrance. Tung Tin is the name of the mountain where it is grown in Taiwan. This type of tea originated in the Fujian province area in China, and the name means "black dragon" in Chinese. TO BREW: Bring fresh water to a boil; let it cool for 5 minutes. Use 1 teaspoon of tea per 8 ounces of water. Let steep for 3 to 5 minutes. The leaves can be infused a second time.

茶王

KING'S TEA: Ellen says this tea is very popular among the Cantonese as a gift. Ginseng comprises about 3 percent of the tea, lending a sweet aftertaste to the green oolong, which is fermented here at 30 percent. TO BREW: Let the water come to a boil and then let it cool for five minutes. Use 1 rounded teaspoon of tea per 8 ounces of water. Let steep for 3 to 5 minutes. The leaves can be infused a second time.

FULLY FERMENTED BLACK TEA:

The time period spent in direct sunlight and fermenting is longer for these teas. By far the most common teas sold worldwide, they're called black tea in the West, but the Chinese call them red teas because they are reddish in the cup. Mark recommends that black teas be drunk in the afternoon, as they have a gentler form of caffeine than green tea and you won't have trouble sleeping.

PU-ERH: Hailing from Yunnan province, Pu-erh tea can be heavily fermented or aged to produce its rich flavor. Known for its ability to aid digestion and help lower cholesterol, Pu-erh is often served at dim sum. TO BREW: Let the water come to boil then use 1 teaspoon of tea per 8 ounces of water. Let steep 3 to 5 minutes. The leaves can be infused a second time.

普洱

祁門紅茶

KEEMUN: 100 percent fermented, robustly flavored black tea, cut into small pieces. Named after the place it is grown, it is considered the best of all black teas. TO BREW: Let the water come to boil, then use 1 teaspoon of tea per 8 ounces of water. Let steep 3 to 5 minutes. The leaves can be infused a second time.

BLACK ROSE: This blend produces a rich red tea with the delicate, soothing scent of rose petals. Actual rose petals are packaged with the tea. Ellen explains that tea leaves can only keep fragrance for one or two days—that is, without modern vacuum sealing. During the dynasty periods of old, growers and farmers were required to send their best tea to the emperor in Beijing, but could be beheaded if suspected of not doing so. Thus, they developed the technique of transporting tea with the flower petals. TO BREW: Let the water come to boil, then use 1 teaspoon of tea per 8 ounces of water. Let steep 3 to 5 minutes. The leaves can be infused a second time.

玫瑰花茶

Mark tells the oolong legend, "Some say the name comes from the dried leaves looking like a long dragon. But one legend says that there was a tree that was very famous for growing the best oolong tea. Everyone wanted to steal the leaves, so for the protection of the tea leaves the owner placed a snake under the tree, and this snake was black and looked like a small dragon. In China the dragon is a very good animal, a symbol of the emperor. Also, the mountain where the tea grew originally in China is said to look like a dragon. So there are many legends like this about this tea." TO BREW: Let the water come to a boil and then let it cool for 5 minutes. Use about 1 teaspoon of tea per 8 ounces of water. Let steep for 3 to 5 minutes and drink. The leaves can be infused a second time.

TRADITIONAL TEA CEREMONY

傳統品茗

ELLEN CONDUCTS educational tea ceremonies for the public and tour groups around a table in the back corner of the store. Hanging on the wall above her is a carving depicting Lu Yu, the Tang dynasty philosopher who is known for establishing how tea should be prepared and consumed properly. The Chinese ceremony differs greatly from the ritualized Japanese ceremony in that conversation is encouraged among friends and family, with great respect and appreciation for the tea itself, of course. The Liis compare it to a wine tasting.

For this ceremony Ellen has chosen Ti Kuan Yin (Iron Goddess of Mercy), a tea that is 40 percent fermented but not roasted, so it still falls in the green category. She enjoys this type of tea in the morning, finding it nourishing and refreshing.

Ellen begins by filling the tea pot in the tea boat (the bowl under the tea pot) with hot water, for if the pot is hot the tea brews better. Electric kettles are used to keep accurate, constant water temperature throughout the ceremony. ○

ABOVE: Ten Ren also sells Pu-erh tea in hard, compacted "brick" form, which was used for centuries as a way to transport tea for trading along the Silk Route. Ellen points out that tea was a primary source of vitamin C for Mongolians, who moved around a lot. Tea was convenient and not heavy to carry, particularly in this condensed form. Pu-erh improves with age, becoming more mellow and complex. The oldest bricks, sometimes 50 to 100 years old, are extremely rare and expensive. TOP: Tea leaves ready to be picked at Mark's family plantation; called "one heart, two leaf," there are very young leaves in the middle flanked by two mature leaves.

FROM TOP LEFT: 1. After pouring the water out into the tea serving pitcher (which looks like a slightly larger teapot), Ellen takes the bamboo spoon and tea funnel and fills the tea pot two-fifths full. She then fills the teapot with hot water and immediately pours the water out again into the tea serving pitcher. This step rinses the tea leaves and brings the fragrance forth. 2. Next is the first brewing. Hot water is again poured into the teapot (with a splash over the outside of the pot as well to keep it warm) and she lets it steep, covered, 1 minute. 3. While the tea is brewing, she warms up the cups with the liquid from the tea serving pitcher. . 4. and subsequently discards the liquid from each cup. 5. She lifts the tea pot out of the tea boat and rubs the bottom of the pot in

circles on a tea towel to remove the dripping water. The brewed tea is poured into the empty tea serving pitcher. This strains the leaves and stops the brewing process. 6. To fill the cups, she pours the tea over the teacups, lined up in a row, in a constant motion back and forth until all of the cups are filled. This ensures that each cup is evenly blended, and one is not stronger than the others. 7. The tea is served. 8. To experience the tea fully, sip it slowly, enjoy its aroma, and appreciate its flavor. 9. The tea host or hostess can brew the tea leaves five or six times more. With some teas, the tea can still taste good up ten times. Each time you brew, add 15 seconds to the brewing time, and always use the tea pitcher for pouring, as it helps prevent oversteeping the leaves. Ellen points out that with this method you're using the same amount of tea as you would with a large pot, but you can enjoy it longer.

WHERE TO SIP TEA IN CHINATOWN

TEN REN'S TEA TIME, *next door to the tea store at 79 Mott Street,* offers a long list of teas as well as the trendy fruit-infused tapioca bubble teas, shredded ice, milkshakes, and tasty snacks like green tea noodles, ten-lu sticky rice, and plum tea jelly.

SILK ROAD MOCHA, *30 Mott Street,* offers teas and also has the best coffee in the neighborhood, plus an Internet café.

FAY DA BAKERY, *83 Mott Street,* offers everything from Hong Kong–style sweet milk tea to bubble tea, plus a huge array of sweets and savory baked goods.

NOM WAH TEA PARLOR, *13 Doyers Street,* is an old-school Chinatown experience. Go for oolong and an almond cookie.

TEARIFFIC CAFÉ, *51 Mott Street,* offers bubble tea, red tea, Japanese green tea, jasmine, and an exotic combination of matcha agar green tea drinks and virgin cocktails. Snacks include taro pudding, yakitori chicken, noodle soups, and rice dishes.

GREEN TEA CAFÉ, *45 Mott Street,* boasts a variety of bubble, milk, green, and black teas in flavors like coconut, almond, taro, and black plum, plus a number of snacks such as fried turnip, country-style duck gizzards, and condensed milk toast.

TEA GALLERY, *131 Allen Street,* is bit of a walk from the center of Chinatown—in the hip Rivington Street area north of Delancey—but the Hong Kong-expat owners offer a very fine selection of oolong and prized, rare Pu-erh teas and are happy to conduct in-depth tastings.

The original tea dispensers at Nom Wah.

Going to Market

FROM TOP LEFT: 1. Silky chicken, which is naturally black, is boiled in stock to make soup for medicinal purposes. It is believed to aid the lungs and supplement the blood—particularly helpful in the wintertime—and is often given to new mothers and the elderly. Cooking silky chicken in other manners is not recommended, as this game bird is said to be tougher than regular poultry. **2.** Aji Ichiban candy and dried snacks on Mott. **3.** Susan Lin of Lin Sister in the upstairs hallway leading to treatment rooms. **4.** Neon feet announce a reflexology practice. **5.** Dried mushrooms stacked at Po Wing Hong. **6.** Live frogs at S & R Seafood. **7.** Bottle gourds or opo squash. **8.** W.K. Vegetable. **9.** Cordyceps for sale in bulk. **10.** Hung Lee Co. Vegetables, 79 Bayard Street. **11 and 12.** Dried meat treats at New Beef King. **13.** Weighing the bounty at Hung Lee. **14.** Dried fish at Po Wing Hong. **15.** Collectibles and toys sit in the window at 32 Mott Street, which used to house the oldest operating store in Chinatown. **16.** Garlic chives. **17.** 32 Mott Street window display. **18.** Dried sea cucumber. **19.** Acupuncturist Dr. Gong displays his book, *Health and Life*. **20.** Dried fish snacks at Aji Ichiban. **21.** New Beef King on Bayard. **22.** Client records at Lin Sister. **23.** Premium ginseng for sale at Po Wing Hong. **24.** Nancy Ng. **25.** 32 Mott Street. **26.** Sea coconut at Lin Sister Herb Shop.

HERBAL REMEDIES

LIN SISTER HERB SHOP, *4 Bowery, Susan Lin*

SUSAN LIN COMES FROM A LONG LINE—generations upon generations—of Chinese medical practitioners. She grew up learning from family members, then went on to study Chinese medicine formally in southern China. In 1980 she was the first member of her family to immigrate to the United States, and she took the work that she could find, first as a "dry cleaning lady," then as a waitress. As she worked, she studied English. She decided to return to her work in healing after a particularly bad bout of poison ivy. Her face and hands were seriously swollen, but she couldn't afford to go to the hospital and pay for prescription medicine. However, from the time she was a child in China, she knew that honeysuckle could help many dermatological conditions. Plucking some that she found growing near her home, she boiled the flowers, drank the fragrant tea, and applied the remedy externally to her face and hands. Within two hours the pain and swelling had subsided. In 1987, with her sister, Xing Lin, Susan opened Lin Sister Herb Shop in the hope and belief that ancient Chinese medical knowledge could help a great many people who can't afford or don't want to rely solely on Western medical care. Their original shop is at 18 Elizabeth Street, and their second, larger location is at 4 Bowery.

Asked to describe her practice, Susan explains, "Chinese medical philosophy is different than Western. We look at the patient as an individual with a complete connection to the body." For example, "If someone has a headache, the Western doctor might prescribe Tylenol or Advil, and not stick to it to search for what caused the headache. It could be due to nervousness, a cold, high blood pressure, lack of sleep, anemia, PMS, a hormone imbalance. Medications like Tylenol or Advil last a couple of hours, then the symptom repeats, and they can also upset your stomach. Chinese medicine is more focused on the cause as well as prevention through customized diagnosis, medication, herbs,

OPPOSITE: Seasonal soups presented in front of the myriad of herbal storage cabinets.

The staff at Lin Sister. Susan's sister Xing Lin stands at the far right.

and teas. We check your pulse, your tongue, ask you questions and talk to you to find out what your body's imbalance is. It is always your body's imbalance that is the cause of the problem, and the balance can be off in several ways: yin and yang, hot and cold, or damp and dry."

Lin Sister carries herbs in both the whole, dried form and a prepackaged powdered form—which are far easier for the novice to use. The staff divides the daily doses of various packets for you, and all you need to do is make a "tea" with hot water, emptying each packet and stirring (and holding your nose, as they can taste and smell quite strong!). Herbal pills can also be prescribed when indicated, or for your convenience when traveling.

Nutritional advice is often a part of the consultation, as food you eat affects your health. For example, if you have a lot of heat in your body, a sore throat, and a dry mouth, Susan might recommend avoiding spicy and deep-fried foods as they cause more heat. She might prescribe forms of exercise such as tai chi, or ask questions about the person's living environment or the hours that they sleep, as these factors impact your health as well. In fact, many Chinatown residents keep standing monthly appointments with their herbal doctors in order to monitor their bodies and adjust their herbal supplements according to life changes as well as the seasons.

Today, Lin Sister provides herbal consultations, acupuncture treatments, reflexology, massage, nutrition, and colonic hydrotherapy, all under one roof. This is unique in Chinatown and fulfills Susan's dream: "to be able to really help someone in all the different alternative ways."

In the pursuit of longevity, prevention, and rejuvenation, there are hundreds of traditional remedies. "The body comes from nature, so we go back to nature for remedies," says Susan. One of these traditional methods is the making of seasonal soups, designed to support the body according to the environmental and health challenges that each season brings.

The soup ingredients feature plants and vegetables grouped by season. For example, bitter melon is used in the summertime soup as the melon cools your system and clears out the heat. Susan believes that fruits and vegetables are most beneficial to us when used in the season that they themselves thrive in.

Ingredients for the soups are given to the customer in premeasured doses, ready to be cooked in a large pot of water or chicken broth. Susan says it is best to make your own broth, using fresh chicken breast without the skin. The ingredients are boiled for an hour and a half, or until they are tender, adding water or broth if necessary. The soup should serve about four people. Edible ingredients such as fruit, beans, and nuts are left in the broth, while items such as bark are removed before serving.

FOUR SEASONS SOUP

This is a general formula meant to help balance the body no matter the season.

1 & 2. Lycium berry and astragulis

3. Longan aril

4. Chinese yam

5. Chinese barley (coix seed)

6. Lotus seed and lily bulbs

7. Euryale seed (fox nut)

8. Codonopsis

春 SOUP FOR SPRING

As spring brings rainy weather, bacteria, dampness, arthritis, and rheumatism, this soup is designed as a diuretic, to cleanse dampness and heaviness, build up your immune system, ease pain, and relax muscles.

1. Chaenomeles (dried papaya) 2. Chinese barley (coix seed) 3. Pueraria 4. Codonopsis 5. Atractylodes 6. White poria 7. Astragulis

秋 SOUP FOR FALL

As the weather becomes colder and drier, our lungs need more strength. This recipe eases the transition by supporting the lungs, and bringing moisture to your body to prevent colds and dry coughing.

1. Glehnia (adenophora) 2. Sea coconut 3. Fritillaria fruit 4. Polygonatun 5. Lily buds 6. Dried tangerine peel 7. Dried pear

夏 SOUP FOR SUMMER

To combat the heat of summer, this formula helps cleanse, cool, and calm down the body.

1. Chinese white bean 2. Chinese small red bean 3. Lotus leaf 4. Alisma 5. Winter melon peel 6. Red poria 7. Bamboo leaf 8. Rush pith

冬 SOUP FOR WINTER

Short, cold winter days require a formula that helps boost energy, keep the body warm, and increase blood circulation while providing nutrients and battling colds. This recipe provides overall support as winter is a good time to strengthen and restore your body and prepare for the next year.

1. Eucommia bark 2. Astragulis 3. Ginger. 4. Codonopsis 5. Angelica 6. Achyranthes 7. Lycium berry 8. Chinese yam

GONG'S ACUPUNCTURE
14 Mott Street, #3, Dr. James Gong

ABOVE: Dr. James Gong in his office and treatment center. OPPOSITE: A regal five-point deer greets clients. In Chinese medicine, deer antler is used to bolster the yang, and strengthen blood, bone and joints among other things.

DR. JAMES GONG has been referred to as the father of acupuncture on the East Coast. After practicing in Hong Kong, he immigrated first to California, then to New York in 1970 to open the region's first acupuncture practice, as well as an herb shop at 26 East Broadway.

Dr. Gong's education began when as a young man in a Buddhist temple in Hangzhou he began reading and studying old Chinese medical books. Fascinated, he later earned degrees at Ling Nam University in Canton, Beijing University, and Hong Kong Chinese Medical College, where he studied with a famous doctor named Dr. Tang. His early studies at Ling Nam gave him his first influential, hands-on experience. He joined a medical team made up of students and a professor, that gave free medical services to people within a twenty-mile radius of the school on weekends. Their method combined Western medicine with traditional Chinese acupuncture, herbs, and other therapies. He was particularly impressed by the effectiveness of acupuncture during these forays, and it became the foundation for his life's work. He is considered a master of acupuncture, herbalism, and Qi Gong therapy.

Excelling in acupuncture is not simply about learning the techniques and set solutions. According to Dr. Gong, you must also "use your own mind." He gives many examples of this in his original diagnosis and treatments. For example, at one point his wife's cousin was very sick. "At only about forty years old he had no appetite, and his whole body felt soft, like a snake," Dr. Gong recalls. "They checked, and he had no special sickness, but I could see he had lost all of his yang, which acts almost like a male hormone. No yang means no life for a man; he was slowly dying." Using his experience with acupuncture and Chinese medicine overall, Dr. Gong prescribed the placement of hot ginger root heart on a specific point on the bottom of the man's foot for thirty minutes a day. This, he says, managed to save his wife's cousin's life.

Over the course of his career, Dr. Gong's reputation has traveled far and wide by word of mouth, and he has treated an international clientele.

Other colorful clients have included the president of the Ivory Coast, an ambassador to the United Nations, and a Saudi Arabian prince who was in school in Boston, who once flew him to his palace to treat his elderly mother, the queen. Another time he was summoned to Paris by a client's family. The patient had had heart surgery while on

vacation and had been in a coma for ten days, languishing in the hospital. Within ten minutes of receiving Dr. Gong's treatments the patient had come out of his coma. Needless to say, he then became known to doctors in Paris.

There are may things accepted as common knowledge in the West that concern Dr. Gong. One example is the promotion of green tea as a popular health drink. Dr. Gong laments, "Green tea is not that simple. By our medical idea, every body or material has a cold, neutral, or hot system. There are over a hundred different kinds of tea, and they also have different qualities.

"Oolong tea is neutral and is good for everybody. Green tea has a cold quality, and is not good for people who have cold systems. It is only good for people with hot systems. For example, someone who is very sick, has very low energy, their body never sweats or urinates a lot—that kind of person is a cold person and should not drink green tea. Otherwise they risk their life." He also notes, "Most people here don't drink tea, they drink Coke, and it's too cold, so it becomes a fat body country, too much Coca-Cola. It's too sweet and it has a cooling property, therefore the stomach cannot generate enough heat to cut down the fat. The right tea will help break down the fat."

Another example that disturbs Dr. Gong is that "every year in the flu season, seven or eight hundred people die every week, and Americans don't treat it right. It's a simple illness. For example, the temperature inside hospitals and patients' rooms is very cold, and this is very bad for flu patients. Their bodies should be kept warm to make them sweat, and they should have lots of hot soup and sleep. People should not die from that kind of simple illness."

The Chinese government asked Dr. Gong to write a book outlining his life and accumulated knowledge. That book is in Chinese, but he has a manuscript in English that he self-published titled *Health and Life*. It contains extensive information on family care, nutrition, male and female health, sex, and the link between internal "cleanliness" and cancer. As he moves into retirement, he is thinking about combining the two books to give a full picture of his work. ○

(See pages 54–57 for more on the Gong family, in the profile of Dr. Gong's son, Jami Gong.)

南北貨

DRIED GOODS

PO WING HONG,
49-55 Elizabeth Street, Nancy and Patrick Ng

PO WING HONG HAS A STERLING REPUTATION in the Chinese community for quality products, including grocery items, herbs, dried fish, vegetable specialties, and ginseng. On any given day as you enter you'll find proprietor Nancy Ng behind the counter greeting regulars and doling out advice on herbal supplements. Nancy is the third generation in her family to be in the grocery business, which her grandfather first started in Guandong. In the beginning the business concentrated on staples: rice, peanut oil, fruit, vegetables, and dried foods. The lack of refrigeration promoted the use of salted fish, preserved duck eggs, and in winter preserved or dried vegetables. There was no electricity, and kerosene lamps were used throughout most of China. While Nancy was still a child, her father moved the business to Hong Kong, where rice, canned goods, and dried seafood remained the popular items and focus of the business.

Nancy's brother was the first to come to New York and set up shop. She recalls, "In 1977 I emigrated here from Canton. I was still a girl, unmarried, but my brother had come first and he was very busy, so I came here to help him, too. Not many people did this kind of business here in 1973, because the trade was limited. After 1978 or 1979, when Nixon opened up trade, it became easier." With more people being allowed to emigrate, there was more demand for Chinese goods, and more acceptance and interest in the general American population for Chinese food. Imported goods like dried abalone, dried fish, and oysters began to be imported. Once in New York they began to stock Chinese herbs and medicines as well, meeting the demand for such things in the growing population.

Po Wing Hong is both a retail store and a restaurant supply outlet. Nancy and Patrick easily work fourteen or fifteen hours a day, seven days a week. Po Wing Hong also exports as far as the Caribbean,

OPPOSITE: Dried rashers of cured pork at Po Wing Hong.

奇有 白油肠 SPECIAL 5.50 5 /LB.

奇有 肝肠 SPECIAL 5.50 /LB.

2.35 鸭比 2.30

香港 鴻昌隆

大澳特產

LLL梅香馬友
MACKEREL FISH

禮品 買6送4+禮品 買5送3+禮品

$328 $188

優力敏
（加強型）
$100.00 每

8樽裝

正野山花旗蔘

日本禾麻鮑
DRIED ABALONE
$950

吉品鮑(24頭)
DRIED ABALONE
$900

吉品鮑-27頭
DRIED ABALONE
$760

吉品鮑(43頭)
DRIED ABALONE
$540

高麗蔘 高麗蔘 高麗蔘 高麗蔘

LEFT: Dried treasures and dried shrimp: Shelled and ideally bright orange-pink, their sharp flavor is used sparingly to perk up rice, soup, dumplings, and stir-fries. If packed in salt, they must be soaked in water for thirty minutes prior to use. ABOVE: Nancy and Patrick behind the herbal counter.

Europe, Africa, and Central and South America, but they've noticed a pronounced change since China has begun to open trade to other countries, and they are sending less abroad in recent years.

Individuals can call in orders as well, and often do for the harder to find items. Teas, herbal drinks, and herbal pills are becoming more and more popular with American customers, Nancy says, and she has expanded those sections as a result. There are also more unusual orders—one customer was consistently buying large quantities of Yunnan Paiyao, a white medicinal powder. Curious, Nancy asked what he needed it for, and was surprised to discover he was using it to help heal injured horses. Yunnan speeds blood clotting internally and externally. Chinese chefs keep it in the kitchen, as it stops bleeding right away when placed on a cut.

Locals regularly crowd the store, stopping by to purchase ginseng, candies, instant noodles, Chinese crackers, a whole range of sauces, pickled vegetables, dried mushrooms, and rice. Expensive specialty items such as dried scallops, oysters, shark's fin, and shrimp are often used as gifts. All of them are flavor enhancers, almost like using salt or pepper. Patrick says dried scallop has great flavor—"Even Campbell's soup used it as a flavoring ingredient." Behind the herbal counter, Nancy holds court at the heart of the store. She has accumulated her knowledge of the uses for different items from books, magazines, Chinese doctors, and frequently from the customers themselves, relating their experiences. On the following pages are some of the ingredients featured for sale at Po Wing Hong, stacked in large glass jars and lined up along the walls, with thanks to Nancy for her tips on their varied uses.

FROM TOP LEFT: **1.** Birds' nests: Swallow-like birds of Southeast Asia make these nests out of their own spittle. Due to the difficulty in harvesting them, they are extremely expensive in the high-quality white and red varieties. Lower-quality nests are called "black" and are not free of twigs or feathers. Vietnam produces the highest, most expensive grade. Less expensive nests come from Indonesia, where people have learned to breed the birds in houses—making what was once strictly for the rich affordable for the majority. Nancy says that birds' nests are prized for their ability to preserve youthfulness as well as combat heart disease, stomachaches, and ulcers. Chinese actresses are known to have one spoon a day of a sweet bird's nest drink as part of a beauty regimen, to keep their skin smooth. Birds' nests must be soaked before using and are cooked in chicken-based soups or with sugar. (See the recipe on page 139.) **2.** Red birds' nests. **3.** Shark's fin: Dried shark's fin must be steamed or blanched several times before it takes on the correct, noodle-like texture that is found in the soup that is ubiquitous at banquets. (See the recipe on page 136.) You can buy it prepackaged, canned, or frozen and avoid the lengthy preparation process, but it isn't considered as tasty as the (more expensive) dried. It is a delicacy that is thought to be helpful in treating cancer and in supporting the lungs, heart, liver, and kidneys. **4.** Sea cucumber: These sea animals, related to sea urchins and starfish, are hailed in Chinese medicine for their ability to fight infection, inflammation, impotence, and muscle pain, as well as to promote general health. A common dish at banquets, they are soaked, cleaned, and simmered before being used in recipes, where they tend to take on the flavor of the sauce that surrounds them. **5.** Canned abalone. **6.** Abalone: Often served at banquets, abalone is thought to be loaded with nutrients and good for the general health. At up to $1,000 a pound, premium dried abalone comes from Japan and must be soaked extensively to become tender. It is then cooked in a stock of chicken and pork before being used. The canned variety is precooked and shouldn't be reheated very long over too high a heat, as it can become tough. Calmex, one of the better brands according to Nancy, costs around $73 a can. Abalone is used in stir-fry dishes, in congee, or as an appetizer. It is particularly popular during the Chinese Lunar New Year banquet. **7.** Wild Korean Ginseng. **8.** Cordyceps: Cordyceps are actually parasitic organisms that grow wild on the backs of caterpillars. Imported from Tibet, the miraculous, rare fungus

is called winter-worm summer-grass, as it "sprouts" from the caterpillar, resembling grass in warmer months. At $200 an ounce, cordyceps are treasured for invigorating the lungs and kidney as well as for increasing blood circulation—much like Korean ginseng is for chi or energy circulation. Both the dried larva and stroma are ground to be used medicinally. **9. Ginseng:** Korean ginseng is the most expensive variety of this prized root, excellent for general good health, reducing fatigue and stress, and promoting the circulation of chi or life energy in the elderly. Though generally considered inferior to Korean, the most valued Chinese ginseng is that which has grown into a shape resembling a human figure, often harvested in the cooler Manchurian region. The American variety of ginseng, of which the best is generally thought to grow in Wisconsin, is very popular among Chinese Americans as a gift, particularly when returning to China. It has different medicinal qualities from Chinese or Korean ginseng, but is restorative and used as a stimulant and toxin-clearing agent. Wild ginseng is more highly valued than cultivated, as it is usually older and more highly concentrated. Woods-grown, planted in the forest and left to grow up to ten years, falls somewhere in the middle in terms of quality. You can see how old the root is by counting the "living scars" found at its neck and adding two. Dried ginseng is often sliced and made into a tea, but it can be bought in powdered, capsule, and extract form as well. **10. Dried abalone. 11. Dried scallops:** Regarded as a delicacy, these sun-dried golden jewels fetch high prices and come in sizes up to two inches in diameter. Very hard, fragrant, and flavorful, they are soaked or steamed before being shredded and used in recipes. **12. Ganoderma lucidum:** Known as the King of Herbs, reishi, or ling zhi, ganoderma is a fungus credited with promoting longevity. Considered a cure-all, its healing qualities have been connected to anti-inflammatory, antibacterial, and antioxidant effects on the body. It can be bought in capsule form, but in its whole, dried form it is sliced and made into a tea.

8
9

10 11

12

AJI ICHIBAN

37 Mott Street and four other locations

AJI ICHIBAN, a chain from Japan, the store is chock full of unusual sweets, from gel and mochi candies in flavors like lychee and kumquat, to tiny marshmallow "hamburgers" and salted licorice. Aside from the buffet of candies, however, Aji stocks one the widest selection of exotic dried fruits and snacks in the city. The fruit ranges from strawberries, papaya, and salted plum to mango, banana, and cherries. Snacks include rice crackers and seaweed as well as an incredible array of chewy dried fish sticks, some with sesame seeds, and crunchy whole dried crabs and fish as seen in the window on Mott Street.

NEW BEEF KING

89 Bayard Street

NEW BEEF KING is dedicated to one thing: making the tastiest beef and pork jerky in town. Using an old family recipe from Hong Kong, the owner meticulously oven-dries each batch—rotating marinated meat through ovens at four different temperatures, then grilling them briefly with sauce. The result is a jerky that is half its original weight and far juicier than regular air-dried jerky. The best seller is their spicy beef jerky, but not far behind are the zesty oyster flavor and sweet and tangy fruit flavor. The beef and pork also come in a "wet spicy" flavor, cooked in a wok with a spicy sauce. More tender (easier on the dental work) offerings are pork or beef jerky chunks that include a curry flavor. New Beef King's bits of tangy perfection can be had at $13 to $17 per pound. ○

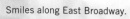
Smiles along East Broadway.

CONDIMENTS

WHILE INCREASINGLY EASY TO FIND in American supermarkets, Chinese and Southeast Asian condiments are widely varied and often absolutely key in re-creating the authentic flavors of a dish. Exploring the aisles of Chinatown grocers has its own appeal; many sauces can be bought premade in bottles, and experimentation can be fun—and sometimes necessary, as labels can be confusing and translations for ingredients vary. Curries, black bean sauce, red bean paste, and chili oils and sauces are easily found bottled, as are dipping sauces for dumplings, hoisin sauce, and a range of light, dark, and flavored soy sauces. ○

SOURCES FOR DRIED GOODS, SPICES, AND CONDIMENTS INCLUDE

ASIA FOOD MARKET, *71½ Mulberry Street*

DYNASTY SUPERMARKET, *68 Elizabeth Street, at Hester*

PO WING HONG, *49-55 Elizabeth Street*

KAM MAN MARKET, *200 Canal Street*

BANGKOK CENTER GROCERY, *104 Mosco Street*

UDOM'S CORP. *Thai and Indonesian Grocery, 81A Bayard Street*

TAN TIN MARKET (VIETNAMESE), *121 Bowery*

1. Canned coconut juice, baby corn, and lychees sit beside various chili sauces, chili garlic sauce, soy sauce, oyster sauce, Thai and Malaysian curry pastes and sauces, and more at Bangkok Center Grocery on Mosco Street. This is the place to find galangal, kaffir limes and leaves, sweet basil, jasmine rice, and lemongrass, as well as dozens of chili sauces, curry, shrimp pastes, and frozen meals. The owner, Premjit Marks, is very friendly and happy to provide recipes and advice on how to make Thai curries, or explain any of the ingredients in her store. 2. XO Sauce is a modern Hong Kong–style sauce made primarily of dried scallops, dried shrimp, chile, and garlic. A tangy, spicy, all-purpose condiment, it is used in everything from pastas to seafood and tofu dishes, as well as a dipping sauce for dim sum. It was named after the well-known brandy, which is highly prized, lending the somewhat expensive sauce a posh appeal. 3. Bags of rice stacked at Bangkok Center Grocery. 4. Shrimp sauce or paste, bottled or dried in slabs can be found in most markets. The pungent smell of the fermented prawn may be a little overwhelming at first, but the unique flavor it imparts is an important ingredient in everything from strong curries to delicate vegetable dishes. 5. Light and dark soy sauce at Po Wing Hong. Generally speaking, the richer dark soy sauces pair best with meats and the lighter sauces with poultry and fish. Both impart color and depth of flavor to a dish.

FRESH FINDS

蔬菜 Vegetables

VEGETABLE SHOPPING, Asian and otherwise, is one of Chinatown's best fresh bargains, be it from a vendor on East Broadway, Canal, upper Mott, or lower Mulberry. Two remarkable (stationary) vegetable shops are Hung Lee Co. and W.K. Vegetable Co.

RIGHT: W.K. Vegetable Co., at 124 Mott Street, has been in business for ten years. Beyond their busy retail business, the proprietor says that they supply restaurants daily, because "people in Chinatown like things fresh." Their wide selection of vegetables are generally available year round, even Chinese specialty greens and lotus root—in summertime, supplies come from Canada and New Jersey, and in the wintertime from California and Mexico. The network of farmers he works with are in large part Asian and often originally from Chinatown, which helps them communicate about the type of vegetables that are in demand there. These farmers own or lease land in Mexico and the United States or Canada and migrate seasonally between their farms. A tour of W.K. reveals a fresh selection of vegetable staples.

FROM TOP LEFT: 1. Bottle gourd or opo squash: Picked when young, these gourds are sweet and delicious in stir-frys or soups. 2. Durian fruit. 3. Winter melon: This imposing melon can grow to up to fifty pounds and can be stored in a cool place for several weeks. Once it is cut into, however, the flesh must be cooked within a few days. At Chinese banquets, winter melon soup holds a place of honor; it is cooked in the melon itself, and the flesh is scooped out as it is served. 4. Taro: Not to be eaten raw, this root tastes like a richer, nuttier potato. It can be cooked in stews or soups, as well as roasted or deep-fried. It turns lavender when cooked, and it's also sweetened and used as a colorful flavoring for bubble tea. The skin contains an irritant, so use gloves when handling it raw. 5. Bitter melon and a variety of greens piled high at W. K. Vegetable, including the delicate, red-tinged "Chinese spinach" called amaranth. In the far corner is Chinese celery, which has a more delicate texture and flavor than American or European celery, and is often used to add aroma to soups and stir-fries. 6. Chinese eggplant: With a sweeter taste, more tender skin and flesh, and fewer seeds than their European counterparts, Asian eggplants do not need to be skinned or salted before cooking. 7. This uniquely warty-looking vegetable is often described as an acquired taste. After blanching to remove some of the bitter flavor, it can be served in a soup or stuffed with strong-tasting ingredients, such as pork or black beans and baked. The very bitter seeds are removed before cooking when the vegetable is mature—though more commonly it is bought and sold green, immature and less bitter. Bitter melon is also known in Chinese medicine for its ability to regulate blood sugar in the treatment of diabetes, or as an antidote for malaria. 8. Chinese chives or leeks: With a mild taste between garlic and onion, Chinese chives are used as a seasoning in numerous dishes, soups, and stir-frys. The more expensive and fragrant yellow Chinese chives are simply Chinese chives that have been shielded from the sun during growth and are used in the same ways. 9. Kohlrabi: Popular in Northern China, this vegetable boasts tender, crispy white flesh that is low in fiber. Often used in stir-fry and soups, it can also be eaten raw. Peel before eating. 10. Napa cabbage or Tianjin bok choy: This cabbage is very common in Chinese cooking, and

can now be found in most American markets. Mild
in flavor, crispy, and tender, it is used raw as well as
in stir-frying and soups. **11. Lotus root:** Very carefully
washed, then peeled and thinly sliced, lotus root is
used in stir-frys and soups. It has a mild flavor and a
firm, crunchy texture. Candied lotus root is given during
Chinese New Year, and both the seeds and the leaves
of this rhizome are used in Chinese cooking. **12. Bok
choy:** Steamed, braised, added to soups, or stir-fried,
bok choy is a very commonly used vegetable. Mild
and sweet, it can be combined with a large variety of
flavorings and dishes. **13. Garlic or flowering chives:**
These are Chinese chives picked just before they flower
and cooked with the buds intact, usually as part of a
larger dish, but they can be steamed separately. **14.
Shanghai bok choy or tong choy:** Shanghai bok choy,
sometimes referred to as Shanghai cabbage, is more
uniformly light green, doesn't flower like bok choy, and
is a little more delicate. It must be watched carefully
when cooking so that it doesn't become overly soft.
15. Choi sum or Chinese flowering cabbage: Choi sum
is tender, sweet, and delicately flavored and is best
steamed or stir-fried. **16. Jicama:** This root vegetable
doesn't have much flavor, but it has a wonderful
crunchy texture and can be eaten raw or cooked.
It's a great alternative to the more expensive water
chestnut, as they too maintain their crunch when stir-
fried. **17. Fuzzy melon or hairy gourd:** Very popular in
Chinese cooking for its mild, sweet flavor; once peeled
it is excellent in soups or stuffing and baking. It's
important that the melon actually be fuzzy or prickly
to the touch, as skin that is too smooth betrays an
older, tougher vegetable. **18. Luffa, Chinese okra, or
silk squash:** A highly fibrous plant, the luffa can be
eaten only when immature, when they are prepared
much like zucchini. Older luffa are skinned, seeded,
and dried, then used as cleaning and bath sponges.

Alongside the vegetable stands are the colorful fruit stands in the neighborhood. Most fruits are recognizable, from the kiwi to the sweet, bright-red lychee, found from May to July. Other finds include papaya, mango, persimmons, pomegranates, plums, and coconuts.

水果 FRUIT

SWEET FRUIT STAND, *Grand & Bowery*

ABOVE: The Fan family has been selling fruit in Chinatown for ten years, starting with a little pushcart on Chatham Square. After 9/11 the business died down and they rented their current location, establishing the Sweet Fruit Stand on the northwest corner of Grand and Bowery. Most of their fruit comes from the wholesale market in Hunts Point, but they buy such Chinese specialties as longan, durian, and lychee from Chinese farmers selling wholesale in the neighborhood. It's a tough business, according to their son, Jason Fan. With lots of competition in Chinatown their prices are kept very low, with margins at tight as $2 on an entire box of oranges, or $1 on a whole box of bananas. In summertime, they carry special varieties of watermelon, green Haitian mango, apple mango, Champagne mango (the variety found in China), and "Santa Claus" melon that tastes like honeydew. You can find yellow kiwi here—the newest kiwi from New Zealand, developed to be more nutritional and sweeter than the original; Jamaican papaya; and persimmons that for optimum taste Jason recommends storing until they're so ripe they seem almost rotten. Hanging prominently along the perimeter of the stand are net bags of the famous durian fruit. One of the most talked about fruits among food fanatics, the durian is well-known for being astoundingly stinky, so much so that in some parts of Southeast Asia it has inspired laws against where it can and cannot be carved. Nevertheless, it is hailed as the King of Fruits, as it has an incredibly complex flavor that is completely unique and very highly sought after. One might taste hints of garlic, cheese, or rotten onion while simultaneously perceiving sweet, fragrant mango, pineapple, or papaya. The flesh is custard-like and smooth. If you prefer not to dig into the fruit itself, you can buy durian-flavored candy at Aji Ichiban, and the Chinatown Ice Cream Factory sometimes features it as a flavor.

1. Durian has a tough, spiked outer skin and a large brown pit, which if properly ripe should move when you shake the fruit. Several slices are made around the fruit, and the flesh is then cut away and packaged for the customer. The plastic gloves offer protection from the strong durian perfume in the rind. 2. The Hami sweet melon comes from western China and weighs three to four pounds. Its flesh is orange-colored and very crispy and sweet. It's in season from June to October. 3. Here Jason's mother takes scissors to cut through to the Durian flesh, which is weaker along the natural lines that delineate its three to five segments. 4. Pomelo or Chinese grapefruit can grow as large as a foot in diameter, with either a yellow skin and pink flesh or a green skin and yellow flesh. The rind is quite thick and takes some effort to peel through, but the sections are easy to eat, as they are less juicy than grapefruit and taste much sweeter. Pomelos are popular during Lunar New Year festivities due to their resemblance to the full moon. 5. A striking and delicious street sweet favored by children, candied longans with a salty-sweet coating are found at a stand on East Broadway. 6. Fuzzy red rambutan for sale on Mulberry Street and at Sweet Fruit. Cousins of the lychee, rambutans and longans are just as sweet and fun to eat. Simply make an incision with your thumbnail and peel away the skin. 7. Slicing through the thin skin of the fanciful dragon fruit, you're rewarded with sweet white or hot pink pulp dotted with tiny black seeds that tastes a bit like kiwi, pear, and watermelon. You can find it from August through November.

肉品市集

MEAT MARKETS

ONE PEEK IN THE WINDOW of Bayard Meat Market at 57 Bayard Street and the Chinese affinity for the swine comes across loud and clear. Every part of the pig is available, from snout to intestine, belly to sparerib, raw, marinated, ground or dried—at excellent prices. Other specialties include fresh (never frozen) poultry, prepared meats in classic sauces, sweet Chinese sausages, beef tendons, Smithfield ham, salted duck eggs, duck tongue, cured and preserved fowl of various dimensions from duck to quail, duck heads for making soup, sweet roast chicken wings, and tripe. For pork fans looking for specialty cuts, at Cheung Kee they butcher three whole pigs on Tuesdays and Fridays.

A SAMPLING OF MEAT MARKETS

BAYARD MEAT MARKET, *57 Bayard Street*

CHEUNG KEE MEAT MARKET, *135-7 Mott Street*

A-FEI MEAT MARKET, *217 Grand Street*

OPPOSITE BOTTOM: Bayard Meat Market Center: Tripe, pork loin, and sea cucumber for sale at Bayard. OPPOSITE TOP: Cheung Kee Meat Market. TOP & BOTTOM LEFT: S & R Seafood on Mott. BOTTOM RIGHT: Crab for sale on East Broadway.

魚類 FISH

FISH MARKETS DOT CANAL STREET and flow through Chinatown, loaded with local and imported selections. Live tanks give the shopper the opportunity to hand-pick lobsters, crab, fish, and prawns. Most of the fish offered is just what you would find at an American market, with the exception of such delicacies as live frogs, sea fungus, and sea cucumber. When shopping for fish in Chinatown, the rule is universal: look for clear eyes, red gills, springy flesh, and a non-fishy smell. Clams should be closed, or should close when you tap on their shells. One advantage at a Chinese fish market is that they typically sell the fish whole to their customers, so it's much easier to determine freshness. They're happy to filet it for you once you've settled on your choice. With the shops being generally open to the sidewalks and exposed to the heat in the summertime, it's best to go first thing in the morning when the shipments have just come in to guarantee freshness. ○

FISHMONGERS TO EXPLORE

S & R SEAFOOD, *135 Mott Street*

82 SEAFOOD CORP., *192 Elizabeth Street*

131 FISH MARKET, *131 Mott Street*

PAN ORIENT AND SEAFOOD CORP., *124 East Broadway*

大型超市 THE MEGA-MARKETS

A RECENT DEVELOPMENT in Chinatown is the appearance of more large-scale market experiences. Po Wing Hong and Kam Man offer huge selections of dried and canned ingredients, with some produce and frozen goods, but there is a new breed that ventures further into prepared foods, bakeries, and raw meats and seafood, following the same trends as the American mega-markets have in recent years. The best of these capture Chinatown in an edited food shopping snapshot, the height of convenience, although they lack the historical romance of the street vendor. The following images showcase the offerings of Deluxe Food Market. This bustling, efficient store runs straight through the block, from Mott through to Elizabeth just north of Hester Street.

With its numerous premarinated meats, bakery, and prepared foods, Deluxe Food Market is engineered toward serving the busy professional, both Chinatown natives as well as the residents of the newly built, high-end condominiums springing up in the neighborhood. It strives to strike the balance between American-style convenience and the food offerings (and low prices) that are still distinctly unique to Chinatown. ○

LEFT: Just inside the Elizabeth Street entrance is a bakery with sweets and bubble tea as well as a hot lunch buffet and seating area. TOP: Mirrored at the Mott Street entrance are freshly prepared hot foods, from pork buns to lo mein, as well as cooked soy and scallion and ginger chickens, prepackaged to take home, and a sushi counter.

MARKETS TO EXPLORE

DELUXE FOOD MARKET,
122 Mott Street and 79 Elizabeth Street, near Hester

DYNASTY SUPERMARKET, 68 Elizabeth Street, at Hester

HONG KONG SUPERMARKET, 109 East Broadway

KAM MAN MARKET, 200 Canal Street

PO WING HONG, 49-55 Elizabeth Street

1. The seafood section boasts premarinated fish as well as freshly filleted. Also available are fish bones for making stock. 2. Butchers stand ready to cut to order. Liver, marinated steak, and chicken feet sit beside tripe, beef shin, and oxtail. 3 & 4. In the center of the store, frozen dumplings and prepacked meats as well as sausages and fresh chicken are found next to a corner stocked with produce.

尋寶之旅

BOUNTY HUNTING

古董、家飾店

ANTIQUES, FURNITURE, AND DECORATIVE OBJECTS

SINOTIQUE, *19-A Mott Street*

Owner Jan Lee collects art, antiques, and furnishings from China, Southeast Asia, Africa, and beyond with a discerning, sophisticated eye. His selections have been featured in lifestyle and design magazines. **(see page 43 for his family profile)**

DYNASTY ARTS, *103 Mosco Street*

Ninteenth-century furniture is featured.

JADE GARDEN ARTS & CRAFTS, *76 Mulberry Street*

A find for pottery, teapots and cups, calligraphy, and incense burners.

Shopping along Canal Street, watches, handbags (though the counterfeits are whispered to you now, post-crackdown), clothing, and trinkets are found in cheap abundance, per usual. But Chinatown has other treasures, within a few steps of the stalls.

禮品店

Souvenir Shops

FOR TOYS AND TRINKETS, there are any number of options as you walk down the street in Chinatown. Below, a couple of the older-style and a couple of the new options.

TING'S GIFT SHOP, *18 Doyers Street*

MAHAYANA BUDDHIST TEMPLE, *133 Canal Street*
On the second floor, they sell Buddhist items, literature, and music as well as a selection of jewelry.

TWINS 99 CENTS PLUS at *Grand Street* sells lots of Japenese imports. Essentially, any toy or small household item that could possibly be made out of plastic is found here in pastel abundance for a song.

傳統服飾店

TRADITIONAL CLOTHING

THE TRADITIONAL CHINESE DRESS, with the high collar, side slits, and heavy silk material, is called a *cheongsam* or *qipao*. In Chinatown, in just a few weeks you can have a fully tailored, handmade one of your own made for around $300 to $400. If that's too rich for your budget, stores do sell them off the rack for much less.

Pictured is Madame Design (or New Age Design) at 38 Mott Street, at the intersection of Mott and Pell. The proprietor, Susan Din, has been creating traditional and nontraditional Chinese fashions for decades now, and will guide you through the design and color combination that perfectly complements your physique.

For inexpensive off-the-rack, try Pearl River Mart, 477 Broadway.

珠寶 JEWELRY

WHETHER IT'S JADE, GOLD, or gemstones you're after, Canal Street and the surrounding area is known for its abundant jewelry stores.

SOME RECOMMENDED VENDORS INCLUDE

GOLDEN JADE JEWELRY, *189 Canal Street*

JADE PARADISE, *85B Bayard Street*

195 DRAGON JEWELRY, *195 Canal Street*

GOLDEN PEARL JEWELRY, *215 Canal Street*

瓷器、廚房用品 PORCELAIN AND KITCHENWARE

KAM MAN MARKET AT 200 CANAL STREET sells groceries, herbs, and candies on the first floor, but go downstairs to find an extremely reasonably priced mecca of Japanese and Chinese porcelain, decorative objects, and teas.○

PEARL RIVER MART, *477 Broadway*

PEARL OF THE ORIENT, *36 Mott Street*, for finer porcelain

街頭小販

STREET VENDORS

Scrolls and fans are found for sale at the edge of Columbus Park, near Bayard Street. Cobblers set up shop along Chinatown sidewalks and work while you wait on a folding chair.

LEFT: Alice Lee has set up her table of jewelry on the Bowery, across from Confucius Plaza, for thirty years now. She has a wide selection of jade as well as some older pieces. Ask to see the finer jade and she will pull it out for you.

TOP & BOTTOM: Fortune-tellers are a common sight along the northern edge of Columbus Park. This one sets up shop at the northeast corner of Bayard and Mulberry.

AVAILABLE FOR PRIVATE EVENTS

第六章 ｜ CHAPTER No. 06

陸

Resources

TRANSPORTATION 交通

NEW YORK'S HISTORICAL CHINATOWN is located on the Lower East Side of Manhattan. It's accessible via subway (6, J, M, Z, N, R, Q, W to Canal; B, D to Grand Street, F to East Broadway) as well as by bus, both MTA (M1, M6, M9, M15, M22, M103, B39, and B51 lines) and private companies. Originally started by entrepreneurial Chinatown residents to satisfy the need for workers and family members going back and forth between Chinatowns along the East Coast, these private companies famously offer the least expensive way to travel between these points. They will deliver you directly to the center of Chinatown for $12 to $20 one-way. ○

TO AND FROM WASHINGTON

Today's Bus (www.today-bus.com)
Eastern Travel (www.easternshuttle.com) Washington Deluxe (www.washny.com)
Dragon Coach (www.ebusticket.com)

TO AND FROM PHILADELPHIA

Today's Bus (www.today-bus.com)
Universe Busline (www.apexbus.com/universe.aspx)
New Century Travel (www.2000coach.com)

TO AND FROM BOSTON

Fung Wah (www.fungwahbus.com)
Lucky Star Bus (www.luckystarbus.com)

Parking in Chinatown can be expensive, and lots are disappearing as new developments are built, but after much lobbying, the city has added meters along Canal Street, which are available for use during evening hours.

TOURIST INFORMATION

THE INFORMATION KIOSK for Chinatown New York City is located at the intersection of Canal and Baxter Streets. Head there for free maps of the neighborhood, event information, and coupon books for shops and restaurants. The kiosk is open seven days a week, from 10 AM to 6 PM weekdays, and from 10 AM to 7 PM on weekends. For more information, including neighborhood tour recommendations, visit www.ExploreChinatown.com.

On the south side of the kiosk is a map of the neighborhood. Areas in red indicate the main sections, where you will find Chinese-run shops and restaurants. ○

Teo Chow (Chiuchow), Beijing, Szechuan

Bo Ky, 80 *Bayard Street*

Peking Duck House, 28 *Mott Street*

The Nice Restaurant, 35 *East Broadway*

Grand Sichuan, 125 *Canal Street*

Southeast Asian

Jaya Malaysian, 90 *Baxter Street*

Sanur Restaurant (Malaysian and some Indonesian), 18 *Doyers Street*

Thái So'n Vietnamese, 89 *Baxter Street*

Thailand Restaurant, 106 *Bayard Street*

Singapore Café, 69 *Mott Street*

Fusion

Almond Flower Bistro, 96 *Bowery*

XO Café, 48 *Hester Street*, 96 *Walker Street*

M Star Café, 19 *Division Street*

Green Tea Café, 45 *Mott Street*

Bakeries and Sweets

White Swan Bakery, 24 *Bowery*

Fay Da Bakery, 83 *Mott Street*, 191 *Center Street*, 214-216 *Grand Street*

Manna House Bakery, 212 *Grand Street*, 125 *Mott Street*, 87 *East Broadway*

Maria's Bakery, 42 *Mott Street*

Egg Custard King Café, 76 *Mott Street*

Chinatown Ice Cream Factory, 65 *Bayard Street*

CELEBRATION

For a schedule of events and festivals:

www.ExploreChinatown.com

Jing Fong, 20 *Elizabeth Street*

Golden Bridge, 50 *Bowery*

Golden Unicorn, 18 *East Broadway*

Grand Harmony, 98 *Mott Street*

Oriental Pearl, 103–105 *Mott Street*

White Swan Bakery, 24 *Bowery*

TEA IN CHINATOWN

Ten Ren Tea and Ginseng Co., 74 *Mott Street*, 138 *Lafayette Street*

Ten Ren's Tea Time, 79 *Mott Street*

Silk Road Mocha, 30 *Mott Street*

Fay Da Bakery, 83 *Mott Street*

Nom Wah Tea Parlor, 13 *Doyers Street*

Tearrific, 51 *Mott Street*

Green Tea Café, 45 *Mott Street*

Tea Gallery, 131 *Allen Street*

GOING TO MARKET

HERBAL REMEDIES

Lin Sister Herb Shop, 4 *Bowery*

Gong's Acupuncture, 14 *Mott Street*, #3

DRIED GOODS

Po Wing Hong, 49-55 *Elizabeth Street*

Aji Ichiban, 37 *Mott Street*, 167 *Hester Street*, 153*A Centre Street*, 188 *Lafayette Street*, 23 *East Broadway*

New Beef King, 89 *Bayard Street*

Fresh Finds

Vegetables

W. K. Vegetable Co., 124 *Mott Street*

Hung Lee Co., 79 *Bayard Street*

Chew Fung Inc., 128 *A Mott Street*

Fruit Markets

Sweet Fruit, *northwest corner of Grand and Bowery*

Hong Kong Supermarket fruit stand, *southwest corner of Pike and East Broadway*

Meat Markets

Bayard Meat Market, 57 *Bayard Street*

Cheung Kee Meat Market, 135-7 *Mott Street*

A-Fei Meat Market, 217 *Grand Street*

Fish Markets

S & R Seafood, 135 *Mott Street*

82 Seafood Corp., 192 *Elizabeth Street*

131 Fish Market, 131 *Mott Street*

Mega-Markets

Deluxe Food Market, 122 *Mott Street, 79 Elizabeth Street*

Dynasty Supermarket, 68 *Elizabeth Street*

Hong Kong Supermarket, 109 *East Broadway*

Kam Man Food, 200 *Canal Street*

Po Wing Hong, 49–55 *Elizabeth Street*

Additional Sources

Asia Food Market, 71½ *Mulberry Street*

Dynasty Supermarket, 68 *Elizabeth Street*

Po Wing Hong, 49–55 *Elizabeth Street*

Kam Man Market, 200 *Canal Street*

Bangkok Center Grocery, 104 *Mosco Street*

Udom's Corp. Thai and Indonesian Grocery, 81 *A Bayard Street*

Tan Tin Market (Vietnamese), 121 *Bowery*

Bounty Hunting

Antiques, Furniture, and Decorative Objects

Sinotique, 19 *A Mott Street*

Dynasty Arts, 103 *Mosco Street*

Jade Garden Arts & Crafts, 76 *Mulberry Street*

Souvenir Shops

Ting's Gift Shop, 18 *Doyers Street*

Mahayana Buddhist Temple, 133 *Canal Street*

Twins 99 Cents Plus, *Grand Street*

Traditional Clothing

Madame Design (or New Age Design), 38 *Mott Street*

Pearl River Mart, 477 *Broadway*

Jewelry

Golden Jade Jewelry, 189 *Canal Street*

Jade Paradise, 85 *B Bayard Street*

195 Dragon Jewelry, 195 *Canal Street*

Golden Pearl Jewelry, 215 *Canal Street*

Porcelain and Kitchenware

Kam Man Market, 200 *Canal Street*

Pearl River Mart, 477 *Broadway*

Pearl of the Orient, 36 *Mott Street*

推荐书單 RECOMMENDED READING AND VIEWING

Anbinder, Tyler. *Five Points*
(New York: The Free Press, 2001)

Blonder, Ellen Leong. *Dim Sum*
(New York: Clarkson Potter, 2002)

Bonner, Arthur. *Alas! What Brought Thee Hither?*
The Chinese in New York 1800–1950
(Madison, NJ: Fairleigh Dickinson University Press, 1997)

Chang, Iris. *The Chinese in America*
(New York: Viking, 2003)

Gong, Rosemary. *Good Luck Life*
(New York: HarperCollins, 2005)

Hall, Bruce Edward. *Tea That Burns*
(New York: The Free Press, 1998)

Kwong, Peter. *The New Chinatown*
(New York: Hill and Wang, 1996)

Kwong, Peter, and Dušanka, Miščević. *Chinese America*
(New York: The New Press 2005)

Leung, Mai. *The New Classic Chinese Cookbook*
(Tulsa: Council Oak Books, 1998)

Lo, Eileen Yin-Fei. *The Chinese Banquet Cookbook*
(New York: Crown, 1985)

Lo, Eileen Yin-Fei. *The Chinese Kitchen*
(New York: William Morrow, 1999)

Moyers, Bill. *A Bill Moyers Special: Becoming American, The Chinese Experience*
(Public Affairs Television, Thomas Lennon, Series Producer, Ruby Yang, Series Editor)

Newman, Jacqueline M. and Roberta Halporn, eds. *Chinese Cuisine American Palate, An Anthology* (Brooklyn: Center for Thanatology Research and Education, 2004)

Yan, Martin. *Martin Yan's Chinatown Cooking*
(New York: William Morrow, 2002)

Young, Grace. *The Wisdom of the Chinese Kitchen*
(New York: Simon & Schuster, 1999)

致謝 ACKNOWLEDGMENTS

AS ONE OF NEW YORK'S greatest and most distinct neighborhoods, the Chinatown section of the Lower East Side is a challenging and fascinating subject—and one that I have been drawn to from the first time I ate dim sum on Pell Street as a child. This ever-evolving community can be labyrinthine in its complexity, and I am eternally grateful to so many members of the community who brought me into their lives and guided me with genuine warmth and enthusiasm.

At the very beginning of my research I had the great fortune to meet Michael Lau and his charming family through a mutual friend, Mr. Ken Cascone. It is impossible to quantify Michael's contributions to this book. Fueled by an intense desire to support his community, month after month Michael made introductions, guided me culturally, shared personal memories, and truly made me feel at home in my adopted neighborhood.

Aik Wye Ng of Explore Chinatown and M. Silver and Associates was passionate in his desire to support the project, and, among many other wonderful people, introduced me to Jan Lee of Sinotique. Jan's passion for Chinatown, past, present, and future, remains an inspiration to me, and I thank him for sharing not only his own story, but that of his father, as well as his personal family albums.

For opening their lives and histories, I am greatly indebted to numerous Chinatown residents, volunteers, and businessmen, without whom this book would not have been possible. Humble thanks to Spencer Chan, Wellington Chen, Frankie Chu, Jami Gong, Jan He, Dr. Herbert Kee, Nancy and Patrick Ng, Father Raymond Nobiletti, Christine and Phillip Seid, and Sam Wong. Many thanks to Mark and Ellen Lii for their supreme expertise in tea; Susan Lin and Dr. James Gong for introducing me to the world of Chinese medicine; Dr. Joseph Lee for his marvelous tours of Chinatown temples; William Chiu for his tour of East Broadway and "Little Fujian"; William Dao of the Museum of Chinese in the Americas; and thanks to Gary Tai of the Consolidated Benevolent Association for sharing the association's collections, including the historical menus and postcards from the personal collection of the CCBA's president, Mr. Eric Ng.

For the delicious recipes in this book, I am ever grateful to Veronica Leung of Dim Sum GoGo; Eric Tsang, manager of Fuleen Seafood; Shanghai Café; Hann Low of Jaya Malaysian; and John Hung of May May. Huge thanks to Tony Liu of *Focus New York* magazine and Toro Associates, who not only shared his story and his contacts in the community but spent hours tirelessly translating recipes from Chinese to English, a true act of kindness for which he refused to be compensated.

Gracious thanks to Georgia Chan Downard, my unrivaled mentor and great friend, for her unwavering excellence in recipe testing and endless encouragement. Thank you to John Michel for his support and insights. And thank you to my family, my koumbari, and Tony Saxton for all their love.

Thanks to Vegar Abelsnes, whose artistic talent shines so brightly throughout these pages—and thanks to his wife Melanie, for patiently putting up with our shooting schedule a mere two weeks after the adorable Josephine was born.

To Judith Regan, whose love for Chinatown was the inspiration for this book, and to whom I am forever grateful for her belief in me. Thanks to art director Richard Ljoenes and designer Timothy Hsu, whose superb vision brought Chinatown to life. Warm thanks to Marta Schooler for welcoming this project to Collins Design. And to my dedicated, patient, and most excellent editor, Cassie Jones, who counseled me from coast to coast and shepherded the book to its full glory: thank you, thank you, thank you. ⭘

INDEX

NOTE: *Italic page numbers* indicate photographs

EXPLORE THE STREETS OF CHINATOWN

1 Mott Street and Canal Street
2 Grand Street and Mott Street
3 Doyers Street and Pell Street
4 Baxter Street and Bayard Street
5 East Broadway
6 Information Kiosk

EXPLORE THE HISTORY OF CHINATOWN

7 Chatham Square
8 Columbus Park
9 Five Points
10 Museum of Chinese in the Americas *(current)*
11 Museum of Chinese in the Americas *(2008)*
12 Church of the Transfiguration
13 Mahayana Buddhist Temple
14 First Shearith Israel Cemetery
15 Edward Mooney House

▣ Subway Stations   **P** Parking lots and garages